Nectar of Nondual Truth

C O N T E N T S

10 Meditation in Vedanta
by Swami Brahmeshananda
Shravana, manana, and nididhyasana — the 3 "proofs of Truth" — reveal themselves as the most important practice in Vedanta in this article. To hear, to contemplate, and then to meditate on the result is the certain way to full understanding leading to realization.

12 The Purpose of Meditation
by Annapurna Sarada
To have a reason to sit quietly surely helps the practitioner of meditation along the inward pathway. Merely sitting in the silence will calm the mind. But other wonders await the apt devotee of God and Truth as levels of ensuing Yoga reveal themselves.

16 Call My Name: A Jewish Meditation Process
by Rabbi Rami Shapiro
A simple, easy, and wondrous way of accessing the indwelling "Spirit" in today's very busy times is through speaking, chanting, and repeating the names of God ardently, with devotion. Many religious traditions, including Judaism, value this practice.

20 Realizing Our True Nature
by Swami Bhuteshananda
A past President Maharaj of the Ramakrishna Order speaks his heart and mind about the need and import of acknowledging and realizing the presence of the "Great Self" within.

25 Eyes Open, Eyes Closed
by Babaji Bob Kindler
A rare and unusual form of meditation that is enjoyed by the pure-minded practitioner or adept is the all-inclusive way of "seeing God everywhere, and in everything." For God will not cease to exist when the eyes open on the world again after deep reflection.

32 Sitting in Ch'an Zen Retreat
by Lex Hixon
Spiritual experiences, strangely enough, are a part of the practitioner's early and late stages of meditation. The middle stages are often quite indistinct. But when these visions, blisses, and insights dawn, they are both exceedingly welcome and wholly undeniable.

36 Meditation on the Breath in Oneness
by Llewellyn Vaughn-Lee
Meditation on the breath is a part of many religious traditions. Often, however, it is seen as an elementary practice used to calm the restless mind. To align it with the life-force forms an entirely deeper echelon, and to actually take a single, fully conscious breath opens up more intense levels still.

40 Meditation & Samadhi
by Swami Aseshananda
The two loftiest limbs of Yoga are explained via rapt discourse by a monastic soul whose practice of meditation spanned over seven decades.

44 Talk with Maezumi Roshi
with Lex Hixon
In an interview with Maezumi Roshi dating from the 1970's, our SRV founder, Lex Hixon, openly and freely discusses the tradition and practices of the Zen Buddhist tradition with a roshi who studied and meditated in both the Soto and Rinzai lineages.

49 Vedanta 101: Spiritual Discrimination
by Annapurna Sarada/SRV Associations
The profound importance of spiritual discrimination, called *viveka* in Sanskrit, is taken apart as to the meaning of attaining the only real and healthy separation that is necessary in the devotee's practice — perceiving the distinction between the real and the unreal, the essential and nonessential, Truth and untruth, God and Matter, Creature and Creator, and so many other false superimpositions that increase the line of demarcation between God and Mankind.

"To know the ultimate Truth on deeper levels of Consciousness is, of course, inspiring and satisfying. To see even a goodly portion of such a vision manifest here on this planet is something many of us are waiting for and have been working towards. As Swami Vivekananda has stated, fervently, *"Oh, when will man be friend to man?"*"

Publisher's Page

Sarada Ramakrishna Vivekananda – SRV Associations
"Setting the feet of humanity on the path of Universal Truth."

Notes on an Advaitic Journal

At the basis of Advaita as the philosophy of Shankara and his gurus, there is Advaita as experience. Advaita as experience represents that supreme place where all diversity merges in its Essence. It is not combatant or immiscible with qualified or dualistic approaches, but rather provides them their place of consummate arrival. Where actual practice rather than mere book learning is emphasized, where religion, philosophy and spirituality are not separate from one another, where knowledge and love, reason and devotion, are never divorced from each other, there does the truth of authentic nonduality effloresce.

Historically speaking, experiential Advaita originated with the ancient Rishis. Therefore, the Upanisads contain the nondual truths of the Vedas which declare: idam mahabhutam anantam aparam vijnanaghana eva, *"This great Being is endless and without limit. It is a mass of indivisible Consciousness only."*

SRV Associations & Universality

The SRV Associations are part of a worldwide movement of spiritual aspirants devoted to the study and practice of Vedanta and Divine Mother Wisdom. The ideals of this ancient pathway to God, exemplified in the lives of Sri Sarada Devi, Sri Ramakrishna and Swami Vivekananda, are the original and eternal perfection of the Soul and its inherent oneness with Reality, the manifesting of divinity in our lives, selfless service of all beings as God, and reverence for the ultimate unity of all sacred traditions. To this end our purpose is to study, worship, and contemplate Truth so that spirituality may flourish. This is the Advaitic way — *"None else but Self, none other than Mother."*

Nectar's Mission — *Advaita-Satya-Amritam*

In Sanskrit, *amrita*, nectar also means Immortality – and this is, indeed, what we are offering: opportunities to become aware of this Amrita that is our very Essence via the rarefied teachings from Vedanta and the World Religions and Philosophies that appear in each issue of Nectar.

Nectar of Non-Dual Truth is SRV Associations' heartfelt offering of highest Wisdom to the human community. It is the sincerest form of love and service we know to disseminate nondual Truth and teachings which transmit pure knowledge, pure love, and true universality. Through Nectar we are working out SRV's mission of spiritual upliftment and education. Please join us; this is a universal movement.

Keeping Nectar in Print

Nectar is a free magazine that can be ordered in printed form online at www.srv.org, and it can also be viewed online. (play.google.com/books) However, substantial donations are needed every year to maintain this publication in print. Why is this important?

1 – Printed Nectars are best for person to person and organization to organization dissemination of these ennobling teachings that deepen one's own spiritual life and engender knowledge of, acceptance, and reverence for all other paths.

2 – Only printed copies can reach those who do not have access to online viewing, including prison inmates, who are a particular focus of SRV's social seva.

Use the subscription/donation form provided at the back of this issue to send a check or credit card payment to SRV Associations, P.O. Box 1364, Honokaa, HI., 96727, or donate online at www.srv.org. Your donations are tax deductible.

With reverent gratitude, we heartily thank the contributing writers of this issue of Nectar of Nondual Truth, who have so graciously and selflessly shared the wisdom of their respective traditions and practices.

Staff of Nectar of Nondual Truth

Publisher
Sarada Ramakrishna Vivekananda Associations
an Annual Publication
For more information concerning the SRV Associations or Nectar of Nondual Truth please contact:
SRV Associations, PO Box 1364, Honoka'a, HI 96727
Phone: (808) 990-3354
e-mail: srvinfo@srv.org   website: www.srv.org
Nectar Subscription is on a donation basis only

No part of this publication may be reproduced or transmitted in any form without permission from the publisher. Entire contents copyright 2018. All Rights Reserved. ISSN 1531-1414

Editor
Babaji Bob Kindler

Associate Editor
Annapurna Sarada

Production
Lokelani Kindler

Cover Image:
Design:
Subhabrata Chandra

Acknowledgement
*Image of Ramakrishna's Disciples
Courtesy of Vedanta Press*
800-816-2242

Contributing Writers
Swami Aseshananda
Swami Bhuteshananda
Swami Brahmeshananda
Rabbi Rami Shapiro
Llewellyn Vaughn-Lee
Lex Hixon
Annapurna Sarada
Babaji Bob Kindler

EDITORIAL

In an issue dedicated almost entirely to the spiritual artform of meditation, *Nectar of Nondual Truth* explores and presents this most needed and necessary facet of spiritual life through the lighted windows of various religious traditions in conscious operation in today's world. Yogic-based eight-limbed meditation upon everything from objects in matter, to the realization of a yogi's conscious Essence is taken up. Meditation on the timeless, beneficial utterance of divine names in a tradition that also favors Reality as nameless, is studied thoroughly by a Rabbi via the Jewish tradition. Then, even the very breath that utters the divine names is inspected in an article on meditation by a teacher in the Sufi tradition. The striking and sobering question asked in several traditions of India, that of "Who Am I," is looked at first hand by an advanced meditator on personal retreat in the Ch'an Zen tradition, who then also takes his place as an interviewer to question a Japanese Roshi about meditation practice in the Soto Zen tradition. Three revered Swamis of the Ramakrishna Order offer up their insights into this superlative examination of meditation and meditator, from different perspectives. Specifically, the very purpose of sitting still and looking within to find the purpose of the entire practice is presented by a long-time practitioner, and finally, an article scrutinizing this most subtle of all yogas from the succinctly nondual position is pondered via the noble Advaita Vedanta perspective. Thus does this age-old and crucial principle of inmost practice — known in Raja Yoga as the singular doorway to Samadhi or Nirvana, — receive a thorough observation from all angles of sensitive, experienced, human awareness.

Widely speaking, for many, meditation is the search for peace in a violent, chaotic world. Others, tiring of the constant variations of the mind/ego complex as it flips repetitively through and between hosts of dualities, daily, take up the practice to still a restless mind. For others, who seek help from higher sources, this precious undertaking called *dhyana-yoga* becomes "....the destroyer of pain," as cited by Sri Krishna in the *Bhagavad Gita*. For the soul dedicated fully to the goal of Enlightenment in this lifetime, the very mind itself is purposefully extracted from the erratic ocean of activities and personal gain and thoroughly doused and drowned in the bliss that is its inherent nature. And so, however one looks upon this spiritual mainstay — as pastime, practice, perspective, or essential principle — its import is incalculable.

SRV Associations loves its work. In whatever way we can be involved in exposing the dharma teachings of the East to the peoples of the West, or even bringing fresh strains of Eastern wisdom back to the East where it originated, we feel gratified to be able to do so. For as our SRV founder, Lex Hixon, often stated, these sonorous teachings of spirituality — so different from the tired tunes of ritual and morality coming from religion, and irreligion — are the only solution for the ills of this world and the ignorance and suffering of its people. Temporary solutions are many, but a single lasting cure....there is but one. When the falsely superimposed line of demarcation between God and mankind is finally erased, then will the Truth of intrinsic Oneness stand forth revealed at last.

To know ultimate Truth on deeper levels of Consciousness is, of course, inspiring and satisfying. To see even a goodly portion of such a vision manifest here on this planet is something many of us are waiting for and have been working towards. As Swami Vivekananda has stated, fervently, "Oh, when will man be friend to man?" We must remain humane, not become insane. So many in the world today are rushing along the ill-considered avenues of greedy accumulation of wealth and goods. The illumined souls of the past did not care for abundance, but rather for freedom from objects and the worries they cause, the distractions they represent. As the great swami wrote in a poem to humankind: "Have thou no home, what home can hold thee friend? The sky thy roof, the grass thy bed, and food what chance may bring — well cooked or ill, judge not. No food or drink can taint that noble self that knows itself. Like rolling river free thou ever be, Sannyasin bold, say —

'Om Tat Sat, Om.'"

Om Peace, Peace, Peace
Babaji Bob Kindler

NECTAR OF ADVAITIC INSTRUCTION

Questions from Our Readers

Divine Mother Reality and Discrimination fill this most recent collection of in-depth inquiries into the nature of Reality, showing that more and more souls are finding the noble Vedanta and, through it, are arriving at the doorway into enlightenment forthwith. Now all that remains is to practice.

"How is Mother seen as permeating all levels of existence?"

She does, as pure, conscious Awareness. How She is "seen" doing this permeation is a secret that only the seers uncover and perceive. She is hidden, Her presence and Essence are most subtle, and She is lightning swift, both in Her actions and Her decrees. When the aspiring soul gets a glimpse of Her, like in the dream state, then more of Her mystery can be uncovered. Until then, meditation, Her mantra, and studying the words of the seers in the scriptures will have to do.....

"After reading and thinking about the explanation of verses 8 and 9 of the Vivekachudamani, how can one address the concept of so-called 'free will'? When saying that Mother is the agent of all action, the creator of all action, and the act itself, then how does individual will and karma fit into all this?"

Individual will and karma fit in when they are surrendered to Her. In the embodied state, with ego and mind manifest, there is no free will; only relative free will. That is, a human being can decide to seek freedom and eschew bondage. That is relative free will. But with all the weights lying upon it, like mind, intellect, ego, thought vibrations, etc., free will is far off. And it gets further away when the soul becomes lost and falls into ignorance and suffering (and into surface pleasures and false happiness).

The soul only really courts freedom, moksha, when it emulates a being who is already free, and that rare soul points them Godward. As Vivekananda has said, "The soul never gets enlightenment from books or temples; it only gets enlightenment from another soul...."

"How can the worldly-minded be shown and convinced that Pure Consciousness exists, and is not a myth or a figment of the imagination?"

They cannot, and one should not waste time trying. If these poor souls see you or I striving and attaining, that will be the closest thing to proof possible. In one of the coming poems you will hear Ramprasad singing *"But this intoxicated poet of Goddess Kali is certain that opinions are void of substance. The Mother's Mystery eludes every earnest practitioner or philosopher who assumes virtue or vice to be real,"* and in fact, that must be the next poem She wants you to take. So remind me to send you that one when you make your next request for one. [this course on Ramprasad poem studies is open to all seekers who are interested]

"In studying the Vivekachudamani, I thought the title for the theme of slokas 4 & 5 could be "Spiritual Suicide Defined." Can you tell me, does *hyatmaha* mean one who turns their back on the Atman, or does it really just mean to commit suicide?"

Certainly, Shankara is not taking up the relative problem of physical suicide. Even today's people do not understand it, and that it has other considerations than say, damnation, attached to it. That aside for now, he is speaking of condemning oneself to lifetimes in maya, on the wheel of birth and death with no knowledge of the freedom available to the embodied soul. Daily life, physical life, sensual life, conventional life, even intellectual life alone – are these true life? Then where is dharmic life, divine life, and the Eternal Life that Christ spoke of?

Where these latter three are missing, then, spiritual suicide is present – even though movement and thinking are still occurring. And so, in the words of the song of India: *"O mind, with eyes wide open and senses fully functioning, you still remain completely blind."*

"In line 5 of the Mother Kali Poem study you sent me, when it reads, 'Your naked and timeless Radiance,' what does 'naked' mean? Does it mean free of attributes or free of fetters? Is it a reference to the Divine Mother's abode in the transcendent Brahman?"

Yes, exactly, It is nondual Awareness, stripped of all attributes and free of all conditions and conditionings. We should all aspire to be more like that.

"How do we cultivate intense faith in the Divine Mother? It would seem that it is a matter of cultivation through discrimination through our every act and the Truth of Her Lila and protection for Her children."

As one grows, so does one's faith. In the West, "seeing is believing"; but in India, hearing is knowing. We have plenty of "irreligion" in this country, but what we need is "ear-religion." The more one hears about Her and Her Wisdom, as well as Her divine sport, the more will one's faith increase exponentially. There is that song of India wherein is stated, *"Before, I never heard of God. Then later I heard my guru calling God 'Mother.' Now I call God Mother too."* This is not a matter of discrimination alone. This is where real Love comes to the fore.

"How does the aspirant 'plunge into union with Goddess Kali?' What steps are to be taken to achieve this? Maybe I should ask instead about the first step that one should take on the road to Reality."

The first step is to yearn for Her, for God. This usually arises when the world fails to fulfill, and the objects in it fail to satisfy. Then the dejected soul turns back towards its Source – which it should never have lost touch with in the first place. Divine Mother awaits, again, for the soul to give up the cheap glass bobbles of earthly existence and begin to assay the gold of Consciousness. There are poems and songs from India that explain this using these kinds of metaphors.

"Does enjoyer devoid of enjoyment mean subject and object have become one? Can you also explain, *'The enlightened one is a yogi devoid of yoga and the absence of yoga,'* please?"

This is one of those particular nondual statements that is trying to explain not only the transcendence of fundamental dualities, but of subtle ones as well. The *Ashtavakra Samhita* and the *Avadhuta Gita* are full of such statements – like, *"Renounce the world, then renounce the poison of renunciation,"* etc. All of this is probably why Avatars like Sri Ramakrishna Paramahamsa preferred to remain in sportive play while in the body, meditating upon Her and taking Her as His Ishta-Devi. But they also used this state to move into formless Samadhi as well, as it is She who so graciously grants access to That – to the experience of Brahman.

"What is the essence of the Guru principle?"

It is the eternal presence of pure, conscious Awareness. If you have read *The Avadhut and His Twenty-Four Teachers in Nature*, you have understood it. The portion at the back of the book on *Guru Tattva* also expresses it well.

"What is meant by the need to realize the Guru in all four states of awareness?"

The Guru is the inner guide, essentially nameless and formless. Since most beings are both attached to and lost in their own waking state, and do not do the "smart thing" and seek out a guide when present there, then they are not apt to do so in the dream state, then certainly not in deep sleep. For instance, you will know that connection has been made to Sri Ramakrishna when, after saying His mantra daily in meditation, and saying it as you fall to sleep, that you gradually begin to have dreams that include Him; otherwise, not. So, one must realize the guru in all four states of awareness. The 4th state is Turiya/Samadhi.

"It seems that whatever the mind attaches itself to (or identifies with) determines our reality in the relative plane. Is this correct? It sounds a lot like the idea, to paraphrase Swami Chidbhavananda, that man is where his mind is. In a nutshell, growing up in the West we have been bombarded with the idea constantly that we are sinners, bodies, individual personalities (egos and reputations), that we live by money not by God, and that gain and loss actually is God in regular life. It seems that all these things involved in the four-veiled pathways serve to keep our minds identifying with relative existence and not with Mother and Brahman. All of this seems to point to the fact that, through sadhana and the elimination of delusional thoughts and behaviors such as fear, doubt, ignorance, selfishness, attraction/aversion of sense objects, we become enlightened right now, while the refinement in the mind occurs culminating in descent of Grace. Is this proper understanding?"

You have it spot on. This is the best writing I have ever read of yours, and the best conclusion. In short, beware of Maya and become aware of Shakti. She will guide humanity up and out of suffering and delusion.

"It is written that the spiritual aspirant must learn to recognize and at once get rid of all negative movements in the mental thought processes so that Mother can bestow Her Grace. Can you please point out these negative movements of the lower nature? Are they worrying, brooding, anxiety, etc?"

Yes, those are some of them. But others that usually come first are wealth, riches, pleasures, and happiness. The soul has to dally awhile with these until they show themselves up to be empty in the end, and unable to fulfill. For instance, the poet/saint, Ramprasad Sen, knows that only Kali can fulfill him. Besides, if he owns nothing and wants nothing, then true happiness is almost his — and he will not have to go through worry and brooding to get to it.

"Do the two powers of Maya, avarana and vikshepa, operate within the two modes of Maya? If so, can we think of avarana as operating both in the individual and the collective or cosmic?"

Yes, the gods, the ancestors — even the Trinity, in some respects — all fall subject to Maya and its two powers. But we need to include the aspect of Maya called Prakasha as well, which is revelatory power. This power of Maya, when operated by The Shakti, can lift veils from even the heaviest circumstances and dullest intellects."

"Is karma the sole agent which dictates one's habits, thought process, and decisions? If so, does this mean that all choices that one makes in this life are predestined by one's karma? If this is true, and everything is predestined, then is everyone just partaking of a predestined path? It seems that one would then be able to have the attitude that 'why does any of this matter?' because everything that is to come and all decisions that are to be made have already been determined by his/her past actions."

Karma is surely the god of this universe, and the ruler of most people's lives. It is not the same as predestination, however, for karma can be both attenuated and dissolved by right action and sadhana. It is not, then, a fixed equation declared by some imaginary power lording over the soul. It is simply an inscrutable outcome of actions done by agents who are not yet free of desire-based works. Most beings, then, are following that activity-dictated path and the mental "grooves" that karma causes called samskaras, and come into life with them. Based upon those samskaras they act within those limitations and form more karma as a result. The good news is that one can free oneself if one understands these truths and applies them, and that "matters," right? It is only in a karma-laden life that apathy and bondage occur, so one must take care to "keep the slate clean" and perform only selfless acts."

"It seems that by following the seemingly cyclic nature of karma, that one can easily adopt a mindset that everything that is to come, and all decisions that are to be made, have already been dictated by one's past actions, so one can thus just 'go with the flow' This also begs the question of why would one want to try and better their karma if this would already be predetermined by their past actions?"

The apathetic, the pleasure lovers, the complacent souls — along with those who have no higher awareness as of yet and see no better way — all follow the flow of karma, satisfied, it seems, with the constant changing of pairs of opposites like pleasure and pain. They do not know the bliss of freedom, or even the exquisite pleasure of a life lived in the dharma, free of weights like stress and brooding. This satisfaction with the status quo is the way of the ancestors, blind to higher possibilities and happy to be in bodies and enjoy the physical senses.

As we found recently, seers like Gaudapada want us to connect to our subtle senses/body, then find the source of our projections in the seeds of deep sleep. Beyond these three states our true nature awaits us, looking on, ever-peaceful, and unaffected by the pains of birth and death and the suffering that accompanies them. As the Avadhuta states, *"I am the fire of nondual Wisdom that consumes the activities of the actionless Atman; I am the fire of nondual Wisdom that removes the sorrows of the sorrowless Atman; I am the nondual Wisdom that dissolves all the bodies of the bodiless Atman. I am Pure Existence, Wisdom, and Bliss, as boundless as the sky, infinite like space. I am the fire of nondual Wisdom that eradicates the sins of the sinless Atman; I am the fire of nondual Wisdom that renders extinct the attributes of the attributeless Atman; I am the fire of nondual Wisdom that strikes off the bonds of the unbound Atman. I am Pure Existence, Wisdom, and Bliss, as boundless as the sky, infinite like space."*

"How does one know that God is God when in human form? e.g., how do we know Sri Ramakrishna is God?"

We know, firstly, by seeing the absolutely singular nature if that man. He was completely given to God. *"Meditating on Brahman, one becomes Brahman,"* say the Upanisads. It is no great secret, but few prefer God to the world. We see few beings so God-intoxicated and God-centered. Is that unfortunate? Yes. But it also marks and accents the presence of such a being among us. With so many ignorant beings around, so many unenlightened ones, it should emphasize the few who appear, right? Well that is what has occurred in the Great Master's case. He is a great Light even among great lights.

Secondly, we know He is God in human form by the company that gathered around Him — His amazing spiritual family. Great luminaries were attracted to Him, as well as authentic devotees. In a short time He has amassed a family of millions. This is not a flash-in-the-pan gathering, but will go on and escalate over time. That is one significant sign of an Avatar's presence on earth.

Third, He brought a Great Ideal to earth in this incarnation, namely, The Divine Mother of the Universe. No one else had ever done this. He is *"Matri bhakta, Yuga Avatar,"* as one song written about Him states. He is the Kali Avatar. Another song states that *"....gods and goddesses revealed themselves to Him in multitudes."* Whether in form, or in the formless state, He was Master. *"The world has never seen a soul like Him before."*

Finally, He revealed and established Universality, and He did so via the nondual way of Advaita Vedanta by realizing Nirvikalpa Samadhi. His many samadhis were legion, and are now legend. He has shown us that samadhi is our true nature.

"How does one make the distinction between a high philosopher and an Avatar? (e.g., Plato vs. Christ/Buddha, etc.)"

Great Souls are not involved in vocations like philosophers are. Instead, they are always freeing souls from bondage to bodies, conventions, attachments, and the like. Their only occupation is awakening God in others. The absence of pleasure-seeking is also a distinction, and a complete disinterest in worldly things and the everyday matters of this earth that engage and compel others. Fully committed disciples attend on these great souls, while savants and the like only get a small following on a secular level which lasts only one lifetime, if that. These are a few of the differences.

"Can you explain a bit about how we want the best of 'becoming' and the best of 'being' for doing service of God in mankind, and how this will lead one to realization of Brahman? This concept was brought out in Swami Ranganathananda's commentary on the *Isa Upanisad*."

This is a good thought. Normally the Vedantist, especially the nondualist, would go beyond "becoming" and adhere to pure "being." Becoming is transformation, and thus untrue. Swami Ranganathanandaji was an exceptional personage. The two times I met with him, in person and alone (the second time being when he was President of the Order) he was so encouraging to all that SRV was involved in, and what we were doing. He told me that spiritual organizations like SRV are rare in this world. We are grateful to him.

Pure Being has obvious advantages, spiritually speaking, but attaining the best of "becoming" is also a great thing. Service of God in mankind itself is some of the best of that, for all whom we serve are caught in the realm of becoming, and the thoughts, acts, hopes, and aspirations of all these are also framed by the realm of becoming. Rare is the being who has given up desire for worlds and objects, who wants nothing more from the world of becoming, and only wants to merge.

Service, worship, spiritual practice, attaining peace of mind — these are all the best of the realm of becoming. Attain them, then "Rest in Peace." Perform all remaining actions from that selfsame Peace.

"When the mind goes down negative pathways due to samskaras, is it a good practice to just point the mind somewhere else (more agreeable) and put effort in not allowing the mind to revisit the negative pathways? A thought that has formed

in my mind is that this practice could be considered a practice of just ignoring the negative tendencies in the mind instead of handling them. On the other hand, I can see how this practice may be in line with the 'watering the flowers and not the weeds' teaching, in that by constantly pointing the mind on agreeable things when it goes down negative pathways the 'weeds' (i.e. negative samskaras) will eventually die off (hopefully). Can you please comment on this and advise if my understanding is acceptable?"

Those whose minds try to ignore deep-rooted problems by simply thinking of the positive do not get far, and that is because they either do not have a path and a teacher to guide them through the tough times, and/or do not keep the practice of positive thinking going long enough so that negativities of the mind actually die and never resurface again. It is not like if I have a negative karma coming up, that I can do away with it by simply pretending it away for a day or two. First one sees and admits it, then one faces off with it, then one does the prescribed practice over a substantial period of time that finally rids one of that tendency for all time. Only those who have persevered in such a regimen succeed in it. All others feign for a time, then return to their old ways. Such tendencies may disappear with the changing of the gunic cycles, you see, and the foolish think they have surmounted the problem. But they return, sometimes with twice the force.

"I understand the value of a spiritual community, but how does one avoid the undesirable effects that can arise in groups. For example, organizations develop politics, group thinking/conforming to conventions within the group, have money/status connected to members, etc. How does one guard against things that may lead to narrow-mindedness within a particular group, and what would be the argument to stay with one community vs. being a sort of 'gypsy' that is part of many spiritual communities?"

This may be why the Divine Mother has kept SRV small. There are no power struggles; nor are there politics of the kind that are not aimed at the highest good of the entire family. Otherwise, and in other groups, such problems come up. This is due mostly to arrogance on the part of independently-minded westerners who know nothing of spirituality yet. Opportunistic charlatans also muddy the waters. They may even call themselves "paramahamsas" and have famous books that teach occult powers to their followers.

Briefly, where dharma is taught instead of pleasure/heaven-seeking, and where austerities (tapas) are accented rather than weakness and dependance, and where the Principle is taught rather than the personality — there you will find safety from the ills of organizations and their power-hungry leaders.

"In terms of Brahman and Atman, is there a distinction/difference between living and non-living solid objects? e.g., do non-living objects in the gross world have Atman, or are they part of Brahman?"

Interestingly, both living and non-living objects are insentient, yet both have Atman as their basis. That is, a rock and the human body are both insentient, both consisting of the five elements, and both having no consciousness of their own. Matter infuses the former, and prana animates the latter, but sentient Awareness is the common underlying substratum for both. Thus, Reality is not a form, but all forms would not appear if Reality were not present. Of course, the mind is the matrix here, which is why we looked into the three states of human Awareness at the recent retreat. In Eastern Yoga psychology, unlike in Western science and biology, the terms sentient and insentient are thought of quite differently. In India, only Consciousness (Chaitanya) — pure, conscious Awareness — is sentient. All else, from the causal to the subtle to the gross, borrows its appearance of sentiency from That, like the moon borrows light from the sun though it appears to shine by its own light. Take the mind away, like in deep sleep, and the world disappears. That is consciousness they are trying to ex out of the equation, but they, themselves, would not be able to think and act without It. The many worlds would not exist without It. Thus, the seers meditate upon It and realize Samadhi/Nirvana.

"Can you please explain how Swami Vivekananda's 5-fold definition of Maya has added to our understanding of Maya? It would seem like, since Maya is actually undefinable, that Swamiji is really talking about the evidence, aspects, or effects of Maya rather than trying to define it? Maybe define is not a good word to use here?"

Maya is inscrutable, not undefinable. Words can suffice almost perfectly as a way to explain Maya, but only if the intellect is refined and some foresight and open-mindedness is therefore present. By slimming his definition of Maya down to a *pancha* teaching, or fivefold, he has — like Sri Ramakrishna did on other topics — destroyed age-old doubts and misunderstandings around Maya. Otherwise, and before he showed up in the West, lesser teachers from India were already on the scene, calling Maya "illusory." But he said "...*it is a statement of fact!*" (read his discourse about maya in his *Jnana Yoga* book). If he had not clarified this, people today would either 1) be thinking all of existence to be illusory (rather than just temporal and changing), or 2) thinking that Maya cannot be understood at all, and so not even trying to espy it and get out if it.

What a service he did for us, then — we who had not the slightest idea that Maya's game was afoot, and that it was lodged in our collective throats like a deadly thorn or cherry pit."

"During our recent retreat together you mentioned that sadhana is how one neutralizes their karma. Does this mean that one is only able to perform sadhana if his/her past actions have led to this effect?"

Yes, as mentioned then, sadhana is the cutting edge way of freeing oneself in this lifetime. One is only able to perform sadhana if one feels bound in any given lifetime and then struggles to get free. It is the Divine Mother of the Universe who bestows upon such a one both the desire to get free, and the will to do sadhana in any given lifetime, followed by the precious boon of a guru and such practices as the mantra and the scriptures. This is superlative, incomparable, and a rare boon that arises due to one's good nature and karmas coupled with the will to be free, *mumukshutvam*.

"I just wanted to share a topic that I have been contemplating for some time now. The topic is regarding the various practices and attainments of the spiritual aspirant (viveka, vairagya, shatsampat, mumukshutvam, etc.). It is becoming apparent that the attainments of the spiritual aspirant, when taken to their highest level, are really different aspects of Brahman. For instance, when vairagya is taken to its para vairagya state, the adept has successfully realized Brahman — for Brahman IS Detachment (or put in another way, Brahman is that state where there is no attaching/detaching to be done, thus is the very essence of Detachment). Also, the attainment of inner peace, when taken to its ultimate level, brings the adept to realize Peace itself — which is how true inner peace (the Peace which passeth all understanding) is achieved, for as long as one is in the realm of the 3 gunas, ultimate peace is always "fighting" with rajas and tamas. These thoughts which came to my mind resulted in the conclusion that all of the practices/attainments of the aspirant are really practices of trying to be one's true nature, and the attainment of that true nature (which one always is, has been, and will be). Is this thinking in the right light? All of these thoughts rushed upon the mind all of the sudden, but seem to make sense.

Yes, all of this recent insight is correct, and on point. In this light the aspirant is heading towards a state that is supremely natural, wherein all is Brahman, yet all that is obviously faulty is thereby null and void. Natural connections (*samhitas*) are recognized at these concurrently ascending levels/states of awareness, and the supremely natural state (*samanvaya*) has returned. Practice will turn into spontaneous living in the Truth, and Dharma. But the practitioner should not jump there too soon. He/she must make sure that all bases are covered — all rocks overturned and every corner of consciousness is looked into and inspected. Then one can proceed accordingly. Give it time...whatever time is needed....to arrive fully intact and in possession of Truth once again."

"I reread the talk 'Maya and Freedom,' as you suggested, and will reread 'Maya and Illusion' most likely tomorrow. When Swamiji states that Maya is 'a statement of fact,' was the main reason then to shatter the ignorance around the matter and thereby remove the misconception of people who think they can deny the world while still lacking possession of Knowledge of Brahman, or even Ishvara?"

Yes. Otherwise, even astute philosophers will misunderstand, and come up with the conclusion that "emptiness" means null and void. True emptiness really clears the mind of clutter so that it can revel in the fullness of its own nature. This marks the difference between Abhava Yoga and Mahayoga in Tantra.

"A follow-up question is, when we study the teachings about Maya, while there are so many facets and difficult to grasp concepts therein, what would be a simple and accessible way to put things to both simple-minded and intellectually astute people so they can become aware of Maya's influence in their life and begin to attenuate its negative aspects? Here is the answer that comes to my mind: 'Maya insinuates Itself on our mechanisms through five aspects: name, form, time, space, and causation. The mind at various levels assigns these to our experiences, thereby creating various divisions, thereby apparently fragmenting the not-two Brahman, causing forgetfulness of It.' Further, it would seem that the following statement could be said in terms of yogic practice and Maya: 'The practice of the Four Yogas utilizes Maya in its revelatory aspect to quell all distinctions and unify experience, resulting in one-pointed mind followed by direct spiritual experience.' Would you agree with these assessments?"

Yes, you have made some good summations here. But no matter how deep or clever the words, people who hear or read them still do not awaken from maya, or even become aware of its presence — not until the Lord, or The Mother, calls them and makes it possible to do so.

"We had a great discussion this evening regarding karma and its workings in the waking and dreaming states. This discussion led to the following questions: How does the law of karma operate in the dream state? Can one accrue karma in the dream state? Lastly, how does the law of karma differ in the waking and dreaming states?"

As for your questions on karma, you have heard the saying that "thought is father to the deed." In this way we certainly set ourselves up for all that we experience in life, and dreaming has a part to play in this. But this is by way of envisioning only, and not by real cause and effect. That is, conceptually, we are prepared to experience what is to come, and the pleasure and pain that accompanies all and everything.

Real cause and effect, however, specific to the waking and dreaming states, operates in such a way that all manifestation are borne out in the waking state. We cannot create karma in a dream, per se; we can only bring it into potential. Acting on it drives it into our lives as real experience. Sri Ramakrishna used to say that so long as one does not act on what one thinks about, then karma will not settle in. In this age (Kali Yuga) one could think about, say, a murder of another person, but so long as one does not carry it out, no karma will come from it (in a subtler age and at a finer level of consciousness, this may not be the case).

Relatedly, this same law follows suit in the life and death states, or bardos, and with earth and heaven. One can neither create nor work out karma in heaven; this is all done on earth, in the waking state, in the physical body. It is by coming to earth, into an incarnation, that people work out their karmas, and this karma was formed on earth in a previous lifetime and body. If you think about it, it makes sense. One does not go to another plane of existence, do some action there, then come back here to work it out. Heaven, or the dream state, is a kind of temporary break from all that. It is in the physical that both takes place, i.e., the formation of and the working out of all karmas — though, as I said, the inventing or conceiving of it all is fathered or birthed at a finer level of existence. Of course, the finest level of existence is karma free.

So, this makes earth, life, and the physical body both very precarious, and extremely important. If it were otherwise there would not be this push for illumination and the search for the path to Enlightenment. We must be "up and at em" and "on vigil" all the time in this regard, which means that living a life of hazy thinking and unconscious actions must be put away forever if we would be truly Free.

Please share this teaching transmission around karma and reincarnation together, and bring it up on retreat as well. The main teaching chart I am introducing there has these elements as several of its important topics for discussion and understanding.

"How can more than one Avatar be on Earth at the same time if Brahman is one without a second? (e.g., the Trinity)"

When more than one great soul comes to earth simultaneously, they are not many; they are always one. It is only others who say "look here, and look there; there are two; there are many." From the standpoint of a realized soul, they see sameness everywhere, at all times. They live in that singular state, therefore there is only one reality. To be more specific, the earth does not exist for them, and they do not "come to earth." They are always in Brahman. Earth is a part of the mind, not of Brahman. When they perceive the earth, it is nothing other than Brahman, so there is no difference. But they do hold the power of discrimination nonetheless, and that helps them stay on the straight and narrow and avoid the detours that maya can create.

"There are often parallels drawn or pointed out between relativity and Reality to help us understand concepts. For example, when Swamiji refers to the wavelengths of light, and how when the wavelengths are very short or very long, we cannot see them with our instrument of sight and there is darkness (only when they fall into the visible region of the spectrum can our eyes sense). This is an analogy for how the absence of thought in a stone and in God are very different things, just like the darkness at either end of the spectrum. Another parallel that is drawn is to explain how everything occurs in circles; just like stars and planets are formed from nebulae and then return to nebulae at the end, we come from God and to God we return. I enjoy these analogies. The question I have is, to what extent should we refer to Physics, since it is ultimately unreal? The predominant theories and models of Physics change over time (as would be expected in Maya, I think). For example, the picture of the Universe has evolved from one that is eternally static with the Earth at the center, to one that arose from nothing out of the Big Bang (some of the Big Bang models have all matter ultimately returning to that single point of origin, so occurs in a circle like above), to our current model that it is and will expand infinitely and is accelerating as it does. I know we are to recognize all of this as unreal, occurring in Maya/relativity, and ultimately transcend it. Can we use our understanding of relativity as a weak gauge that might point us to Truth? Is there value in seeing the limits of Physics and, by that, knowing there must be something beyond?"

Not just value, but real necessity — even urgency for the soul bound into matter. The world is a hole in the ground, filled with ignorance, disease, decay, suffering, and death. No serious thinker, lover, or meditator would hold on to it, what to speak of turning it into the only reality. Reading the signs that it points to, such as the presence of infinity, forms the makings of a way out of it once the soul has identified with it and been born in the very womb of it. Name, form, time, space, and causality; that is maya. Those five also happen to be five of the best principles to meditate upon. But one must know them to be ever-changing as one does. Otherwise, the soul ponders them and gets stuck in them. As Sri Ramakrishna has stated, fittingly and revealingly: *"The more lives in ignorance one lives, the more one begins to believe that the world is real."*

"In SRV we speak of taking mental postures rather than mere physical ones. Is taking the mental posture, 'I am meeting Kali now,' recommended for one such as myself, or is it premature? If the latter is the case, what postures should we take to qualify ourselves for such an exalted 'mental position?'"

Sincere practitioners ought to put thoughts and ideals like this on the mind like a coat. Then see what occurs. But do not let the ego handle that coat; take it off the hook of Mother's toolshed using the two hands of the devout heart and nondual mind, then place it over your thinking process with the refined intellect. Then, as I say, watch what happens.

"What is the best thing that one can do to help the suffering that exists in this world? It is my understanding that the best thing one can do is to become enlightened, as this will remove one's contribution to the collective ignorance that exists and then one is fit to actually help remove the sufferings that do exist from a higher standpoint than the world. For how can one really help the suffering that exists in the world by means of the world?"

Of course you are right. But until that most sublime of moments dawns, the best one can do is to attempt to see through what they call the illusion of suffering, the illusion of death, and even the futility of immature compassion. The immense strength and unbridled boldness that we saw in Swami Vivekananda was due to the absence of all forms of weakness, certainly of the mental variety as well. The word "undaunted" does not do justice to his forthrightness and forward motion. He often used to say that most beings who take up the body are meant to suffer. That means, that not only is it in their karmas to do so, but that some souls even prefer to suffer. What can we do, in our naivety, for those who would rather we not help them — particularly when most of us know next to nothing about how to really help another soul, and whereas our "help" would probably make matters worse for them if we tried?

And so it goes. We strive and learn, gain strength and clarity, then finally take our place among those who know the nature of Reality to be beyond all contrasting pairs of opposites — like pleasure and pain, life and death, and ignorance and bondage. For only then, with Them, can we be truly effective in the singular spiritual art-form of work as worship, and labor as love, free of any motive whatsoever — even free of what we think is best for others based upon their ultimately unreal pains and sufferings and the real reasons they have to suffer them.

Questions, observations and insights regarding problems in spiritual life or the issues of the day may be directed to Nectar's editorial staff at srvinfo@srv.org and will be duly addressed in succeeding issues.

◆ SWAMI BRAHMESHANANDA

MEDITATION IN VEDANTA
To Hear, To Ponder, to Realize

In the tradition of Advaita Vedanta, Truth is one and indivisible, but the ways and methods utilized to reach That ultimate Goal are legion. In the path of meditation this proves true as well, as contemplation with form, meditation beyond form, visualization using objects in nature, and cogitating upon noble ideas in the mind, are all valid means for reaching union with the blissful, transcendent Brahman.

What is *Vedanta*? In some circles all the religious ideas of Indian or Hindu, or to be more precise, Vedic in origin, are considered Vedanta. Although it may be true in a general way, this statement must be carefully understood and specified.

The word, *"Vedanta,"* literally means "the end of *Vedas*" or "the essence of *Vedas*." *Vedas* are considered to have three broad sections: The largest first portion is the *Karma-kanda*, or the work portion, which deals with the rituals and sacrifices of various types. The second part deals with various *upsanas* or worships. The third and the last part of the *Vedas* deals with Self-Knowledge and consists of the *Upanishads*. While the teachings of the *Upanishads* could be interpreted in dualist as well as monistic, or for that matter in many other ways, generally the word *Vedanta* is used in the monistic or *Advaitic* sense. Sri Shankaracharya has in one sentence beautifully summarized the essential teaching of *Advaita Vedanta*: "Brahman, or the Supreme All-Pervading Consciousness, alone is Real. The world is illusory, and the individual soul and Brahman are not different." (Brahman Satya Jagat Mithya; Jivo brahmaiva na parah) All Vedantic meditations are based on, and centered round, this ultimate truth.

Vedantic Meditation: The Crucial Three Steps

In *Advaita Vedanta*, meditation is called *nididhyasana*. In fact, it is a three-step process. The foundation of this meditation is by careful, serious, and faithful study, or better still, the listening of the *Vedantic* texts from an adept and learned preceptor who has at least to some extent realized the *Vedantic* truths. This step is called *Shravana*, or listening. This also includes carefully ascertaining the ultimate unity of existence, or *Brahman*, as one without a second. The aspirant carefully reasons on what he/she has heard or read with the help of reasoning based on the scriptures. The second step is called *Manana*, which means constant thinking of the same truth. The third and the final step is *nididhyasana*, or meditation, in which the stream of same ideas, to the exclusion of all other dualistic ideas, is maintained uninterruptedly. These three should not be considered separate, for the first merges into the second, and the two into the last.

The first step in *Vedantic* meditation is to decide via the process of *shravana, manana,* and *nididhysana*, or hearing, reasoning/cogitating, and meditating, "Who am I?" I cannot be the body, for body is an object and I am the subject. I am the witness, and the body is seen by me. The body is constantly changing and will ultimately die, while I remain constant and am immortal. These are just a few reasons presented. *Vedantic* texts teach us these facts in much greater details. These must be repeatedly heard, reasoned, and meditated upon until we actually start feeling that we are not the body. After this, the same process is employed for the vital forces in our body, for the mind, for the intellect, and even for the ego. All these are to be negated by this three-pronged *Vedantic* process of meditation.

Once the individual is able to clearly feel, through this long time process of meditation, that he/she is not a body-mind complex, but rather is Pure Consciousness, then one must meditate upon the identity of his/her individual Pure, Conscious Nature in conjunction with the All-pervading *Brahman* Consciousness with the help of meditation on Great *Vedantic* dictums like "Aham Brahmasmi" — I am Brahman, etc. Sri Shankaracharya explains the process of this meditation in his classic scripture, *Vivekachudamani*. Here are some examples:

"That which is beyond caste and creed, family, and lineage, which is devoid of name and form, merit and demerit, that which transcends space, time, and sense-objects — That Brahman art Thou. Meditate upon this in the mind.

"That Supreme Brahman, which cannot be comprehended by speech, but is accessible to the eye of pure illumination; which is stainless, the embodiment of knowledge, the beginningless entity — that Brahman art thou. Meditate on this in thy mind.

"That which is untouched by the six-fold wave (viz. decay and death, hunger and thirst, grief and delusion, which overtake the body and mind); meditated upon by the yogis in their hearts, but never grasped by any sense organ; which the buddhi or intellect cannot know — That unimpeachable Brahman art thou. Meditate on this in thy mind." (Vivekachudamani, 254-256)

In another type of Vedantic meditation, the Unity of existence is meditated upon by the same threefold process. There are a number of pots and toys, like elephant, mouse, bird, etc., made out of clay. If we negate the name and form we shall find that they are all, in fact, only clay and nothing else. Similarly, according to *Vedanta*, all objects in the world have name and form, and they exist, are manifest, and are dear to someone. If we, by reason, discard the names and forms, which are the cause of differentiation, the one, pure, Absolute Consciousness remains. Just as by knowing the clay, all objects made of clay are known, just as by knowing steel, all objects made of steel are known, similarly, by knowing the one, Pure Consciousness, which is the Essence of everything, everything is known.

> "Just as by knowing clay all objects made of clay are known, and just as by knowing steel all objects made of steel are known, similarly, by knowing the one, Pure Consciousness, which is the Essence of everything, everything is known."

While the meditations described here employ the threefold process of hearing, reasoning, and meditation, there are also *Vedantic* meditations involving the process of visualization, aimed at the ultimate Goal of Unity or Advaita. One may consider the Absolute Reality, or *Sacchitananda Brahman*, as an ocean, and oneself a fish joyfully sporting in it. In a slight modification of this meditation, one may consider the soul as an earthen pot dipped in the ocean, with water within and all around. Next, one thinks that the pot has broken and there is nothing but water all around. Yet another envisionment, centered round the ocean, is to consider the All-pervading Absolute Consciousness as the ocean, and all souls as bubbles and waves. An incarnation of God is like a big wave.

One may also envision the Absolute, All-Pervading Consciousness as the formless sky, and one is a bird flying freely in it. Light, too, can be used for meditation. Consider that all around, everywhere, there is one indivisible Light of Consciousness, and that individual souls are like sparks of light. Now consider that the sparks are merging in the Absolute Light.

Objective and Subjective Meditation

There is another way of looking at meditation in *Vedanta*. There are two kinds of meditation in *Vedanta*, viz., the objective and the subjective. In the objective meditation the ideal is regarded as outside, and in the subjective meditation it is inside the meditator. The objective meditation is, again, of two kinds, according to the ideal as associated with or conditioned by a sound symbol (*shabdanuviddha*), or by a form symbol (*drisyanuviddha*). The meditation associated with a sound symbol consists in repeating such formulas as "*Om Sacchitananda Brahma*," or "*Om Sacchidekam Brahma*." The former means "*Brahman is Absolute Existence, Absolute Knowledge, and Absolute Bliss.*" The latter means "*Brahman is Reality, Consciousness, and the One without a second.*"

In the objective meditation, associated with or conditioned by a form symbol, the aspirant meditates on some object or form that seems to him closest to *Brahman*. Every object is a combination of the Absolute and the relative. In everything one finds not only existence (*Sat*), cognizability or knowledge (*Chit*), and attraction or bliss (*Ananda*), which are the different aspects of *Brahman*, but also a name (*nama*) and a form (*rupa*), which are the traits of the phenomenal world created by ignorance (*avidya*) and therefore illusory. While meditating on a form symbol, the aspirant should gradually withdraw his mind from the unreal name and form and concentrate on *Brahman* which is present in the symbol as Existence, Knowledge, Bliss Absolute. In and through the objects he should see *Brahman* as one sees the ocean in and through the waves.

The objective meditation has its *savikalpa* and *nirvikalpa* aspects. In the former, the aspirant is conscious of the object of meditation, viz., *Brahman* associated with a sound or form. But as the meditation deepens he attains to the *Nirvikalpa* state, and the entire phenomenal world disappears in *Brahman*, and the aspirant becomes one with That.

In the subjective meditation, the ideal is placed within oneself, and the heart is considered a very suitable place. It is considered like a lotus bud with a subtle luminous space within which is considered the abode of Brahman. As the aspirant progresses, he realizes that the heart denotes not only the physical organ, but the *buddhi* or intellect. Hence, *Brahman* is described in the *Upanishads* as residing in the "*cave of the buddhi.*" Finally, he transcends both the heart and mind and realizes *Brahman*, the All-Pervading Consciousness, in his inmost consciousness.

As in the objective meditation, so in the subjective meditation, the ideal may be associated with a sound symbol or a form symbol. In the former, the aspirant repeats a *Vedic* aphorism such as "*I am Brahman*" (*Aham Brahmasmi*). In the latter, the aspirant observes that there arise in his mind such forms or ideas as desire, determination, doubt, belief, nonbelief, fear, etc. He meditates on the Consciousness which is the witness of these forms. This subjective meditation, too, has its *savikalpa* and *nirvikalpa* aspects.

By means of meditation, subjective or objective, and through gradual steps, the aspirant attains Self Knowledge in *Nirvikalpa Samadhi*, a state in which all mentations cease. He experiences Supreme Bliss. "*All fetters of the heart are cut asunder, all doubts of the mind are dispelled forever, and he becomes free while living — a Jivanmukta.*"

A former editor of the Vedanta Keshari, and previously of the Ramakrishna Mission Home of Service, Swami Brameshananda is a senior monk of the Ramakrishna Order and until recently was the Secretary of the Ramakrishna Mission Ashram in Chandigarh, India. Over the years his writings in Hindi and English have appeared in several journals, including Prabuddha Bharata, Vedanta Keshari, and Nectar of Nondual Truth. He specializes in themes related to Jainism. He is now retired and is living in Varanasi.

◆ ANNAPURNA SARADA

The Purpose of Meditation
& Connecting the Eight Limbs of Yoga

Swami Aseshananda once stated, *"Meditation is feeling the Presence of God."* Over the decades that he served as Minister of the Portland Vedanta Society, he gave innumerable insights regarding the nature and practice of meditation, but this is the one I return to again and again. Concentration on that deceptively simple statement immediately reverses the trajectory of the outward-going mind and lifts the veil over an intuitive awareness of a changeless Presence – the Seer, the Divine, one's own Self – the Witness of changing phenomena. But intuitive awareness, as helpful as that can be initially, is only the beginning, a bare glimpse.

The Eight Limbs of Yoga (systematized by Patanjali nearly 2000 years ago from practices millennia old), even in their simplest presentation, provides a very clear path for practice. Considering all eight limbs starting from the goal, *Samadhi*, one develops an idea of what is needed to achieve it, and why the first steps are so important We might be tempted to skip steps if we are not aware of the Grand culmination that awaits, and its connection to the other limbs.

The 8th Limb – Samadhi, Absorption

Samadhi is divided into two categories: Seedless and Unseeded. *Asamprajnata Samadhi,* also called *Nirvana* in Buddhism and *Nirvikalpa Samadhi* in Vedanta philosophy, is the indescribable absorption in Ultimate Reality – Existence, Knowledge, Bliss Absolute – the One without a Second. It is called a "seedless *samadhi*" because all causes are burnt via this supreme transcendence. These causes are the seeds for action, for bodies (whether physical or subtle), for objects and worlds. *Asamprajnata Samadhi* is the Peace that passes understanding. And lest one fear the loss of one's individuality, we have only to look at the blissful countenance of Sri Ramakrishna or Ramana Maharishi, and note how their lives were spent trying to share this supreme secret with others – humanity's own true nature!

Then, there is Swami Vivekananda's statement that we are not individuals yet! (CW, vol 2, p. 80) We have mistakenly invested our sense of individuality in all that changes: senses, body, mind, intellect, ego – all limitations on our true Individuality that is all-pervasive, indivisible, Free, and untouched by time, space, and causation. The ancient Seers of India realized, and then stated, that one who knows *Brahman* (the Ultimate Reality) becomes *Brahman*. This Knowing is not in the objective sense of subject and object; language cannot state it directly, being dual by nature. "Knowing," here, is the transcendence of Subject-object awareness.

Asamprajnata Samadhi is attained rarely, only after all *samskaras* and *karmas* are transformed via the seeded *samadhis*, which are states of absorption that retain the experience of Subject and object, bliss, and "I-ness."

The other category, *Samprajnata Samadhi,* also called *Savikalpa Samadhi* in Vedanta philosophy, are "seeded" *samadhis*. In this *samadhi*, the sense of individuality is retained as one has not transcended the sense of an individual self and otherness. *Yoga* divides this limb into four kinds, ranging from those having one-pointed intellectual inquiry on gross and subtle objects, to those that retain the purified ego in the (finite) bliss of absorption in the subtlest cosmic principles. Further explanation is beyond the scope of this introductory article and requires a qualified teacher. [see page 30] But we know from the great teachers of *Yoga* that repeated practice of these seeded *samadhis* dissolves *karmas* and transforms *samskaras* (inherent tendencies from previous lifetimes that influence one's thinking and actions) into *samskaras* for *samadhi*. Patanjali states that one of the obstacles to *Yoga* (*Asamprajnata Samadhi*) is attachment to subtle bliss. He is referring here to these seeded *samadhis*. Attaining them is no small feat, but ultimate Freedom lies beyond. These *samadhis* are not attained without the ability to enter into true meditation.

The 7th Limb – Dhyan, Meditation

The word "meditation," as it is commonly used, generally refers to sitting quietly with eyes closed and trying to attain calmness. In *Ashtanga Yoga,* the 8-Limbed Yoga of Patanjali, meditation refers to a state of one-pointed concentration that is maintained for a certain length of time. It has been likened to the way oil appears when it is poured from one beaker to another. It is a smooth, continuous flow without any splashing. Sri Krishna likens it to the appearance of a candle flame kept in a windless place, i.e., one would not know, if looking from a distance, if it is a real flame or the picture of a flame. In true meditation, the effort to avoid distraction has been transcended. Time exists only as an idea there; the ego takes a back seat. If one maintains this meditation, it transforms into one of the seeded *samadhis*; and if one abandons attachment to the states of bliss and desire for the *siddhis*, occult powers, the gate can open for *Asamprajnata Samadhi,* the pure state of *Yoga*.

Meditation depends on the ability to concentrate the mind without distraction.

The 6th Limb – Dharana, Concentration

Concentration is essential to the practice of Yoga. The intermediate practitioner will spend most of his or her time in formal practice trying to keep the mind steady on a single object of thought. Patanjali states in sutras 1:31-2 *"Grief, mental distress, tremor of the body, irregular breathing, accompany non-retention of concentration. To remedy this, the practice of one subject (should be made)."* He then offers up different kinds of subjects to suit various temperaments. [see chart on page 15]

Very importantly, Patanjali made use of *Sankhya's* 24 Cosmic Principles – from the element earth to unmanifested

> "In true meditation, the effort to avoid distraction has been transcended. Time exists only as an idea here; the ego takes a back seat. If one maintains this meditation, it transforms into one of the seeded samadhis."

Prakriti/Nature – calling them *alambanas*, supports for concentration/meditation. [see box below] In waking and dreaming consciousness, our mind is ceaselessly engaged with gross (physical) and subtle (mental) objects. While awake, we use our external senses to experience external/gross objects. While asleep, we use dream/subtle senses to experience dream/subtle objects all conjured by the mind. The intellect and ego drive both these kinds of experiences via desire and aversion. The 24 Cosmic Principles are the materials of waking and dream experiences. In dreamless sleep, where cognition ceases, all these principles return to their unmanifest state and wait to repopulate the dream and waking states.

Sankhya's 24 Cosmic Principles
Categories of Nature, the non-Self

Prakriti: Insentient Nature, intangible matter-energy consisting of the Gunas in equilibrium. The 24 categories evolve from Prakriti, from subtle to gross:

1 - *Mahat*, Cosmic Mind
2 - *Buddhi*, Discriminitive Intellect
3 - *Ahamkara*, Sense of Separate Self
4 - *Manas* - Mind
5 - 9 - *Jnanendriyas*, Cognitive Senses (hearing, touching, seeing, tasting, smelling)
10 - 14 - *Karmendriyas*, Active Senses (speaking, handling, walking, procreating, excreting)
15 - 19 - *Tanmatras*, Subtle Elements (audibility, tangibility, visibility, flavor, odor)
20 - 24 - *Panchamahabhutas*, Gross Elements (ether, air, fire, water, earth)

Since we are habitually, serially, concentrating on gross and subtle phenomena in an uninformed and unaware way, one of the ways of stabilizing awareness that Patanjali suggests is to concentrate on these alambanas in specific ways that, first, reveal their existence to us, and then gradually unlock their real meaning, exposing our attachment and/or aversion to them, their impermanence, and ultimately, our freedom from them. This process convinces the practitioner that the Self/Seer is not the seen: not objects or senses (whether waking or dream), not even the mind and ego, and not the material source of all these, *Prakriti*. Yet, in the course of practice, one realizes that all these have come out of the mind at cosmic, collective, and individual levels. Thus, this is not a practice that dismisses and alienates one from nature, but one that shows the interconnectedness of everything while the ever-free Self looks on, unaffected.

Concentration is not possible without the ability to withdraw the senses from their objects, and the mind from the thought of objects, except that one to be concentrated on.

The 5th Limb – Pratyahara,
Withdrawing the Senses and Mind from Objects

This is the pivotal Limb between the lower and higher limbs of *Yoga* and shows to what degree one's mind has been purified by practice of Limbs 1 - 4. The practice of concentration referred to above is a matter of taking one object for concentration and leaving off all other objects. *Pratyahara* is the qualification for it. It requires that one has the developed the will to detach, which depends on cultivating discrimination between the stationary Self and everything else, dispassion of mind, nonattachment to the objects and relationships of the world, and freedom from a chaotic lifestyle brought about by disturbing *karmas*. This is the practice that gives us control over distraction so that concentration can be held long enough to develop into meditation, so that meditation can be held long enough to develop into samadhi. [see article on page 25 of this issue]

Patanjali describes the five states of the mind-field as being scattered/*kshipta*, dull/*mudha*, gathering/*vikshipta*, one-pointed/*ekagra*, and dissolved/*nirudha*. Only the last two are fit for Yoga. The third one, which describes a mind that is alternately focused and then distracted, is fit for practice. The first two are harmful and require purification via the first two limbs.

The 4th Limb – Pranayam, Control of the Prana

Pratyahara is possible when the *prana* is under one's control. Physical *prana*, called vital force, circulates throughout the body causing food to be digested, lungs and heart to pump, sense organs to operate, and other functions. These can all be controlled, meaning that the prana can be made to flow smoothly. Psychic *prana* is the force that impels thought, memory, desire, emotion, and reaction. It is ultimately the psychic *prana* that yogic practitioners must control in order to achieve *pratyahara*, *dharana*, and the rest. Beginning practices start by using the breath to recognize the presence of *prana* as vital force and discover one's ability to control or guide it. The fact that one uses one's will – a mental effort – to do this, reveals the connection between physical and psychic *prana*. Commonly, people say "thought is father to the deed," but they often take that connection and what it implies for granted.

In most people, the physical *prana* does not flow smoothly, causing disease or discomfort, and this affects the mind. Those lacking moral and ethical discrimination are unable to restrain the action of the senses, and come under the influence of anger, jealousy, lust, greed, desire for enjoyments, etc. The *yogis* who have mastered both physical and psychic *prana* use the psychic *prana* to regulate the physical prana. This is natural and effortless; for a calm and peaceful mind leads to physical health and right action.

The 3rd Limb – Asana, A Posture Suitable for Meditation

To practice *Yoga*, one must be able to sit still, undisturbed by the body. Movement of the body distracts the mind. Pain in the body also distracts the mind that is not fully under one's control. Though *hatha yoga* prescribes many kinds of *asanas* for bodily health, Patanjali's *Yoga Sutras* are concerned with attaining meditation and samadhi, and only one posture is necessary, preferably seated on the floor, in a position that allows the spine and neck to be naturally and comfortably upright, the diaphragm to move freely, and which can be held for a long time. This often takes practice if one is accustomed to slouching; the muscles that hold the spine erect have to be strengthened, hip and leg muscles need to be flexible. If necessary, a chair can be used. Most important of all is the will to undergo these practices with the right orientation. Engaging in *yogic* practices based on the desire for physical health, beauty, admiration, wealth, and power, will not lead to *Samadhi*, rather, away from it. Right orientation is developed via the first two limbs of *Yoga*, the *Yamas* and *Niyamas*.

The 2nd Limb – Niyama, The Five Beneficial Practices

All the other limbs of Yoga depend on this and the next Limb, for they represent the foundation of one's character and the right orientation needed to purify the mind. Their observance and practice, or lack thereof, result in good, bad, and mixed *karmas* that help or hinder one's pursuit of true *Yoga*. The five *Niyamas* consist of: austerity/*tapas*, purity/*saucha*, contentment/*santosha*, self-surrender (of the fruits of one's actions) to God/*Ishvarapranidana*, and recitation and study of scripture/*svadhyaya*. Patanjali has singled out three in particular as exceptionally important: *tapas*, *svadhyaya*, and *Ishvarapranidana*. Purity and contentment will certainly flourish if one performs austerity, destroys ignorance of the real nature of one's Self via deep and daily study of Wisdom scriptures, and surrenders the ego at the feet of God or an illumined Soul. The desire and capacity to follow such practices requires a firm moral foundation, strong will, detachment, and a more or less neutralized *karmic* slate. All too often, students set their foot on the spiritual path only to be blindsided with various *karmic* upheavals. Someone whose attachment to the world prevents them from maintaining a balanced mind in the face of loss (or gain) – of work, of loved ones, of health, wealth, and other challenging events – and thus blames God, devil, or others, cannot successfully tread the path of *Yoga*.

The 1st Limb – Yama, The Five Observances

Neutralizing one's *karma* begins here. The *Yamas* consist of nonviolence/*ahimsa*, truthfulness/*satyam*, noncoveting/*asteya*, continence/*brahmacharya*, and non-acquisitiveness/*aparigraha*. Behaving opposite to each of these is due to unchecked desire and selfishness, which lead in turn to negative *karmic* events, compounded many times. Ideally, one should be born with these five virtues already established. If one's life is a roller coaster of difficult events, then these virtues, along with the *niyamas*, should be observed with intense diligence combined with non-reaction. Passionate reactivity to the events of life only conduces to more of the same. To neutralize *karma*, it is imperative to let events rise and fall and hold to the *yamas*.

Yoga is often described as the union of thought, word, and action. Each *yama* is to be observed in all three ways: in action, in word, and finally in thought, the last being increasingly possible as the mind increases in purity. Adherence to these is of grave and utmost importance. They should be exemplified by parents, school teachers, and leaders of society. Our children will be saved untold suffering if they are taught to maintain these from childhood.

Siddhanta, Conclusion

In conclusion, let us return to the goal: feeling the Presence of God/attaining *Samadhi*. Swami Vivekananda, who brought the teachings of *Vedanta* and *Yoga* to the West in 1893, wrote, possibly, the first English translation of the *Yoga Sutras* for the Western people, called Raja Yoga. He was breaking new ground in a culture unaccustomed to thinking of religion in terms of Realization, and unfamiliar with the existence of *prana* and subtle matter, *tanmatras*. Looking out upon the people of Europe and America, and not seeing anyone who had attained these higher states of *samadhi*, he took great care to teach this system in as simple a way as possible. It is fervently hoped that more and more people embrace this universal system and attain peace, concentration, meditation, and *Samadhi*.

"*Samadhi is the property of every human being.... Each one of the steps to attain Samadhi has been reasoned out, properly adjusted scientifically organized, and, when faithfully practiced, will surely lead us to the desired end. Then will all sorrows cease, all miseries vanish; the seeds for actions will be burnt, and the Soul will be free forever.*"
– Swami Vivekananda in *Raja Yoga*, Complete Works (C, vol. 1, p. 188.

Annapurna Sarada is the president of SRV Associations and an assistant teacher for the sangha members and their children. She also writes on spiritual topics at Medium.com. To read more about SRV's children's classes and retreats, visit the newsletter archive on SRV's website: www.srv.org

The Seven Methods For Mastering Awareness
With Vedavyasa's Commentaries on Yoga Sutras I.33 – I.39

1. Parikarmas
The Four Refinements

"Cultivate friendliness towards those who are happy, compassion for the sufferers, appreciation for the virtuous, and indifference towards the non-virtuous. The mind thus becomes pure and, purified, it attains stability."
— Vedavyasa on Sutra I.33

2. Vidharana
Conscious and Even Breathing

"As an aid for establishing greater stability of the mind, the practice of the expansion of the breath and the prana is duly recommended and utilized." — Vedavyasa on Sutra I.34

3. Vishayavati Pravrtti
Contemplating Objects

"By focusing on the nostrils, tip of the tongue, palate, middle of the tongue, and root of the tongue, perception of the subtle nature of smell, taste, form, touch, and sound occurs. Celestial bodies and objects are also known by this special concentration. Via this method of direct experience, doubt is dispelled, the teachings of the seers and acharyas get accepted, and the gateway to wisdom and samadhi opens." — Vedavyasa on Sutra I.35

4. Vishoka Jyotishmati
Meditation on Inner Light

"Practicing meditation in the heart-lotus, the buddhi reveals itself and appears clear and luminous, like a sun-filled sky. From the comprehension of this ocean of sorrowless Light, calm and serene, springs the great realization, 'I Am.'" — Vedavyasa on Sutra I.36

5. Vita-Raga-Vishaya-Chitta
Contemplating Divine Beings

"By contemplating and reflecting the mind-fields of perfected sages and seers who have transcended all attraction for the sense objects, the yogic practitioner gets free of attraction and attachment and gains the state of stability." — Vedavyasa on Sutra I.37

6. Svapna-Nidra-Jnana-Alambanam
Recalling Dream Experiences

"The yogi also attains the state of stability of mind when he contemplates in profound meditation the states of dreaming and deep sleep." — Vedavyasa on Sutra I.38

7. Abhimatadhyan
Meditating on a Chosen Ideal

"Overall, the yogi may allow the mind to meditate upon whatever is most pleasing and beneficial, for through this method as well the mind also becomes stable and enters samadhi." — Vedavyasa on Sutra I.39

"To overcome the impediments to Yoga and other distractions, recourse to the one-pointed practice of a single method is enjoined. As concentration occurs, knowledge of all things, from gross to subtle, is gained, and samapatti, mastery over the mind-fields, is attained." — Lord Patanjali

Chart by Babaji Bob Kindler — Property of SRV Associates

RABBI RAMI SHAPIRO

CALL MY NAME
A Jewish Meditation Process

There are numerous contemplative practices in Judaism, but one figures most strongly in my own daily practice: *gerushin* or what we might call *nama–japa*, repeating the names of God.

Gerushin is a Hebrew word meaning "to separate:" to separate oneself from falsehood, illusion, delusion, and *mochin d'katnut*, the narrow mind of the egoic self, and open us to *mochin d'gadlut*, the spacious mind of God. In this essay I explore the practice using texts from the Hebrew Bible.

God Called "Light" and Light Was (Genesis 1:3)

The world that you and I see is a universe of names. God calls "Light!" and light appears. God separates light from dark and names each. Without names there is only chaos, what *Torah* calls *tohu va-vohu:* "wild and unformed" (Genesis 1:2). Naming is how God orders creation, and how we bring meaning to it.

For example, the first thing that adam (earthling, from *adamah*, earth) does, is imitate God and name the animals: God brings all the animals to adam "to see what adam would call them;" whatever the earthling called an animal would be its name, (Genesis 2:19). Naming is what we earthlings do. It is how we become intimate with life. It is how we make sense out of our existence. Eventually we mistake the name for the named, and create a world almost entirely from words. When the words no longer point to something beyond themselves they become idols. We begin to worship the words and forget that they point to something else.

There is one Name, or one category of Names, that returns us to reality. This category is the myriad Names of God. While it is true that we can use these Names to further our barrier building, and even excuse violence against those we call "other," this is a misuse of the Name. This is taking the Name in vain, something we are expressly forbidden to do (Exodus 20:7). Proper use of the Name leads from the narrowness of fear and barriers to the spaciousness of love and harmony. This use is found in every religion. Moslems chant the 99 Names of God found in the Holy Qur'an. Christians chant the Rosary or the Jesus Prayer: *Lord Jesus, Son of God, have mercy on me, a sinner.* Hindus practice *Nama-Japa* the repetition of Names such as Ram and Krishna. Pure Land Buddhists chant the *Nembutsu*, invoking the name of the Buddha of Infinite Light. Jews chant one of the Names of God found in Hebrew scripture or rabbinic tradition. While it is true that most Jews do not do this, and may no longer recognize *gerushin* as a Jewish practice, it was once normative.

At That Time They Began To Call Upon The Name YHVH (Genesis 4:26)

The Hebrew Bible traces the practice of calling upon the Name of God to the time of Seth, the third son of Adam and Eve. It was the earliest form of prayer. It was simple and concise: just calling out the Name YHVH. No specific posture was needed. No priesthood or intermediary is mentioned. Just you calling to God.

Today Jews no longer vocalize YHVH, and use a variety of other Names instead. Chief among these is *Adonai*, Lord. Sadly, Adonai not only acts as a substitute for YHVH, it erases the true meaning of YHVH in the minds of most Jews. *Adonai* is a noun; YHVH is a verb ("to be"). *Adonai* is masculine; YHVH is more gender fluid. *Adonai* implies hierarchy; YHVH implies holarchy where all things are a part of rather than apart from the Whole that is YHVH. While most English Bibles translate YHVH as Lord, a more philosophically accurate translation is the "Happening happening as all happening."

A far better and no less ancient rabbinic stand–in for YHVH is *HaMakom*, "The Place" in which and of which all happening happens. This is the notion Rabbi Saul of Tarsus referred to when he spoke of God as *"that in whom we live, and move, and have our being,"* (Acts 17:28).

By the time of Abram the practice of calling out God's Name often included building an altar, a focal point for calling the Name. These were temporary structures and did not give rise to a temple or a professional clergy to monitor and facilitate it. Torah says, *"Abram built an altar there (Bethel) and invoked the Name YHVH, and then he journeyed on,"* (Genesis 12:9). True prayer is part of our journey. We call on the Name as we journey on. Spirituality of this kind is simple, portable, applicable everywhere at any time. It requires nothing more than the willingness to call and the calling itself. As the Psalmist says, *"I will sing praises to the Name of the Lord,"* (Psalm 7:17).

I Will Proclaim Your Name (Psalm 22:22)

Gerushin is the practice of proclaiming God's Name. The psalmist is not speaking metaphorically. He means for you to speak God's Name aloud. Proclaiming God's Name is a ceaseless practice. There is no end to it. The Name repeats over and over and over again, permeating your very being. You begin to vibrate with the Name, as the Name. In time you discover you are not proclaiming God's Name, but your name; and not only your name, but the name of all beings: *"For now you are no longer separated from God, and behold you are God and God is you; for you are so intimately adhering to God that you cannot by any means be separate from God, for you are God. See now that I, even I, am God. He is I and I am He,"* (Abraham Abulafia, 13th century kabbalist). Everything is the One Thing; all names are variations on the One Name, YHVH, the Happening that is all happening.

> "Saying the Name of God is pleasant because when you fall into the rhythm of *gerushin*, you are overcome with joy. Just as a baby delights in the babble of its own voice, so will you delight in the ceaseless repetition of God's Name. There is something intrinsically wonderful about this practice. It is fun, joyous, and free from the seriousness of so much that passes for spirituality."

Sing God's Name For It Is Pleasant (Psalm 135:3)

Saying the Name of God is pleasant because when you fall into the rhythm of *gerushin*, you are overcome with joy. Just as a baby delights in the babble of its own voice, so will you delight in the ceaseless repetition of God's Name. There is something intrinsically wonderful about this practice. It is fun, joyous, and free from the seriousness of so much that passes for spirituality. There are arduous practices taught by great spiritual teachers, but *gerushin* isn't one of them. *Gerushin* is easy. There is no sense of mastering anything. You do not get better at the practice. It is just the ceaseless repetition of a Name of God. The challenge is to stick with it.

All Who Call Upon God's Name Will Be Delivered (Joel 2:32)

Delivered from what? From our addiction to the narrow self and the fear-driven living that is its hallmark. Throughout the Hebrew Bible God is forever challenging us to *"fear not."* This challenge occurs dozens of times, suggesting that fear is the greatest obstacle to human flourishing. Deliverance is the deliverance from fear to love, from strife to tranquility, from selfishness to selflessness, from cruelty to compassion, and from wickedness to justice.

Each People Will Walk In The Name Of Its God.... (Micah 4:5)

God is the Source and Substance of all reality; the Happening happening as all happening. Everything is in God and God is everything. If God is everything, than anything can become a Name of God. Yet, there are some Names that have become infused with the power to deliver us from narrow mind to spacious mind. Names such as *HaMakom, Krishna, Ram, Jesus, Allah, Amida Butsu*. These are the Names at the heart of the universal *gerushin*. There is no need to borrow a Name from another people, each has its own. Yet there is a need to find the Name that works for you, the Name in which you can walk.

Finding a Name that speaks to you is critical. You may have to experiment with several before finding the one that is right for you. According to the rabbis, you should choose a Name and recite it for forty days. If you fail at that, the rabbis assume the problem isn't with you but with the name: choose another name and try again until you find one that you can repeat for forty days. Once you've reached the forty day mark, the Name, or so the rabbis taught, is now established in your mind and will not leave you. Here are some of the Hebrew Names of God Jews use: *El* (God), *Yah* (The Ineffable), *HaShem* (The Name), *Ribbono Shel Olam* (Master of the Universe), *Shalom* (Peace), *Shalem* (Wholeness), *HaKadosh* (The Holy One), and *HaRachaman* (The Compassionate One).

My own *gerushin* practice focuses on *HaRachaman*, the Compassionate One. Using this name comes from the Hasidic sage Levi Yitchak of Berditchev (1740-1810) who used it to enter into ecstatic union with God: *"Where can I find You, and where can I not find You? Above— only You! Below — only You! To the East— only You! To the West— only You! To the South— only You! To the North— only You! If it is good— only You! If it is not— only You! It is You, It is all only You!"*

I Will Wait Upon Your Name (Psalm 52:9)

Waiting upon God's Name is to enter into it as you might curl up close to a warm fire on a damp and chilly night. The Name becomes a refuge, a safe haven from the madness of the narrow mind's endless drama of the fearful and alienated ego. The sense of safety that comes with the Name is a gift of grace. You cannot make it happen, you can only wait for it to happen. And when it does, the dis-ease of *mochin d'katnut* vanishes, and you rest in the peace of *mochin d'gadlut*.

What Is Your Name? (Genesis 32:29)

Jacob was the first of the biblical sages to ask God's Name. Alone at Jabbok's Ford, waiting for his brother to come and, he suspects, kill him, Jacob is attacked by an angel of God who may in fact have been God. The angel/God cannot defeat Jacob but does succeed at wounding him in the thigh, causing him to limp for the rest of his life. As dawn approaches the angel demands that Jacob release him. Jacob demands a blessing first. What he receives is a new name, *Yisrael*, "one who wrestles with God." Our given names, the names we receive from our parents, are the names associated with *mochin d'katnut,* narrow mind. When someone calls that name, you turn around to see if it is you that is being summoned. As we mature on the spiritual path we receive new names, names that act not as reminders of who we are, but as signposts for who we strive to be. *Yisrael* is the state of the spiritual warrior that Jacob is to become.

Jacob then asks for the angel's name, and the angel replies, Why inquire after my name? The question is crucial. There are two reasons for knowing God's Name. The first is to chant the Name as a means of surrendering narrow mind to spacious mind and awakening to the unity of all things in the nonduality of God. The second is to use the Name to control others. The history of religion is filled with people who lay claim to special knowledge that they use to exploit those who lack that knowledge. If you want to know God's Name in order to gain power over self, then you are using it wisely. If you want to know God's Name in order to secure power over others, then you are using it unwisely. If you want to know God's Name in order to surrender to God and slip into spacious mind, then the practice of *gerushin* is healing. If you repeat God's Name to bolster the delusion that you (the narrow self) are God, then it is damning. Before you begin chanting God's Name, be clear as to why you are doing so.

The angel answers Jacob with silence. Some commentators believe that the angel ignores Jacob or refuses to answer his question, but this is not so. The angel does in fact answer his question, the answer is Silence.

To You Silence is Praise (Psalm 65:2)

God is beyond naming. No Name, no matter how sacred, can articulate the fullness of the One Who Is All. This is why *Torah's* core Name for God, YHVH, is literally as well as legally unpronounceable. It is a Name that yields only silence. Silence is the Name of God. This silence is not a proper noun, but a state of being. As you repeat your Name you will find that there are moments when the Name simply repeats of itself, and then ceases altogether. This is not a loss of focus, this is the true gift of this practice: both narrow mind and spacious mind grow so still as to leave you enveloped in Silence. In this silence you realize that both *mochin d'katnut* and *mochin d'gadlut* are manifestations of God; that narrowness and spaciousness go together as convex with concave; that you are God whether you realize it or not.

They Shall Walk in My Name (Zechariah 10:12)

Walking and reciting the Name of God is one way to engage in this practice. As Torah tells us, we are to recite these words *"when you walk on your way,"* (Deuteronomy 6:7). There are two aspects to walking. Deuteronomy speaks about walking on your way, and Zechariah speaks about walking in God's Name. Only when the two are integrated is *gerushin* really happening.

Walking on your way means engaging in the ordinary duties of your everyday life. *Gersuhin* is to be totally integrated into your daily life. You are repeating the Name of God as you go about your day.

Walking in God's Name means that you are enveloped by the grace of God evoked by the Name. Your day is infused with grace, joy, love, justice, and humility. You manifest the Name in all you do. This is a special kind of walking. *Torah* calls it *lech lecha*. The phrase literally means to walk (*lech*) toward yourself (*lecha*). *Lech lecha* is a pilgrimage from self to Self, from narrow mind to spacious mind. How do you walk this way? By repeating the Name of God.

God calls to Abram (and to each of us) saying, *lech lecha*, walk out of your homeland, your tribe, and your family (Genesis 12:1). In other words: free yourself from the conditioning and prejudice of nationality, ethnicity, religion, and parental bias. If you can do this, God will show you the land as God wants you to see it: free of the fears and prejudices of *mochin d'katnut*, narrow mind, and radiant with the Glory of God in and as all things.

I Will Glorify Your Name Forever (Psalm 86:12)

"Forever" means unceasingly. This is Rabbi Saul's notion that we should *"Rejoice always, pray without ceasing, give thanks in all situations,"* (I Thessalonians 5:16). *Gerushin* is a practice that continues all day long: As the 18th century rabbi, Alexander Ziskind, wrote in a letter to his children, *"I will tell you, my beloved children, that whenever I was not involved in study or prayer, the words Yotzri u'Bori Ata (You are my Maker and Creator) were ever-present in my mouth and even more so in my thoughts."*

Give Me An Undivided Heart To Revere Your Name (Psalm 86:11)

What is an undivided heart? A heart that is willing to accept the dual nature of the human being. You are both narrow and spacious, both self and Self. When you pit one against the other, you are divided against yourself and cannot proclaim the Name of God.

> "How can you unite your heart? By accepting all that arises within it. Do not reject the unpleasant, nor cling to the pleasant. Do not mistake whole-hearted for half-hearted, and seek to feel only the good, the loving, and the holy. Feelings arise of their own accord. Feel them when they come, do not hinder them as they go."

How can you unite your heart? By accepting all that arises within it. Do not reject the unpleasant, nor cling to the pleasant. Do not mistake whole-hearted for half-hearted, and seek to feel only the good, the loving, and the holy. Feelings arise of their own accord. Feel them when they come, do not hinder them as they go. In this way your heart is undivided, making room for everything and its opposite; realizing the greater unity in which all duality rests. Only this heart can revere God's Name.

Save Me, God, By Your Name (Psalm 54:1)

As the Name becomes embedded in narrow mind it counters and neutralizes the poisons of selfishness, greed, anger, fear, and despair that feed *mochin d'katnut* and make it unhealthy. This is the salvation *gerushin* offers.

Mochin d'katnut is a necessary part of you. You cannot function without it. Narrow mind allows you to nurture and affirm your uniqueness. It allows you to cultivate and celebrate your preciousness. The problem is not with narrow mind per se, but with its tendency to block out the equally necessary insights of *mochin d'gadlut*, spacious mind. *Mochin d'katnut* becomes so infatuated with itself that it cannot bear to realize that it is part of a system of divine unfolding that manifests an infinite array of equally unique and precious beings. It is the narcissism of narrow mind that threatens your sense of harmony and wholeness, and blocks you from realizing your true nature as the image and likeness of God.

Gerushin is the antidote to this narcissism. It does not do away with *mochin d'katnut*, but allows narrow mind to see itself

> *"Gerushin is not a difficult practice. It can be taught as a tool that children can use whenever they are feeling frightened, stressed, angry, or confused. When little children chant the Name of God they naturally find themselves calming down, both physically and mentally. This is the blessing that accompanies their repetition of the Name. As they become still they can see what is happening more clearly and respond to it more creatively."*

from the perspective of *mochin d'gadlut*. In that spaciousness lies salvation: the realization of self and other as God. Salvation is awakening to the preciousness of self even as you realize the interconnectedness of all selves in and as God. With salvation comes an overwhelming sense of loving and being loved. You are suddenly free from the fears that plague *mochin d'katnut*: the fear of failure, the fear of love, the fear of relationship, the fear of death. With the ending of fear comes the freeing of love. Narrow mind is now the vehicle for loving the parts even as spacious mind is the vehicle for loving the whole.

I Will Bless In Every Place Where My Name Is Remembered (Exodus 20:21)

Re-membering is re-pairing: putting together that which was split apart. Your sense of being split off from God is an aspect of *mochin d'katnut*, narrow mind. Since *mochin d'gadlut* is always aware of the unity of all things in and with God, it has no need to remember or repair. The place of remembering then is *mochin d'katnut*. The power of *gerushin* is its ability to engage narrow mind and awaken it to spacious mind. *Gerushin* practice does not erase narrow mind, it liberates it from the illusion that it is the only mind. *Gerushin* frees *mochin d'katnut* from playing God and allows it to realize that God is playing it. This is the blessing that happens in this place of remembrance.

Place My Name Over The Children of Israel And I Will Bless Them (Numbers 6:27)

Placing God's Name over the children means teaching children how to take refuge in the Name through the practice of *gerushin*. *Gerushin* is not a difficult practice. It can be taught as a tool that children can use whenever they are feeling frightened, stressed, angry, or confused. When little children chant the Name of God they naturally find themselves calming down, both physically and mentally. This is the blessing that accompanies their repetition of the Name. As they become still they can see what is happening more clearly and respond to it more creatively. A still mind and body is fearless, focused, and alert. It is ready to do whatever needs doing without the babble of self and selfishness. Teaching *gerushin* to children offers them a skill that will serve them well throughout their lives.

And Speak Them When Sitting At Home (Deuteronomy 6:7)

The "them" in this case is the Name of God. "Sitting at home" refers to formal meditation practice. Make time during the day for formal *gerushin* practice, repeating the Name while sitting comfortably with your eyes closed. According to the *Talmud*, the anthology of rabbinic teachings, the ancient sages used to meditate one hour before and one hour after each of the three daily prayer services. I'm not suggesting you set aside six hours a day for meditation, but making time for formal *gerushin* is desireable.

The Name should be repeated in sets of 101 repetitions. This number comes from a rabbinic teaching that it is good to recite a *mishnah* (a teaching of the sages) one hundred times, but it is better to recite it one hundred and one times. The word *mishnah* means "to repeat," and refers to the rabbinic practice of learning through oral repetition.

When Lying Down And When Rising Up (Deuteronomy 6:7)

Torah urges us to practice *gerushin* as we lie down in bed to sleep, and when we wake from sleep and prepare to go about our day. Repeat the Name as you bathe, dress, and otherwise prepare for the day. In time you will discover that the Name is being chanted while you are asleep and is naturally present to you when you rise up in the morning.

It Is Not In Heaven (Deuteronomy 30:12-14)

For some people, the simplicity of *gerushin* is its greatest obstacle. They prefer something more difficult in order to excuse their failure to do it. This is why Moses taught, *"It is not in heaven, that you should say, 'Who will scale heaven for us and bring it to us?' ... Neither is it across the sea that you should say, 'Who will sail the ocean for us and bring it to us?' ... Rather the Word is very near to you; it is in your mouth and in your heart, (so that you can do it).* The word is the Name of God. It is already in your heart and your mouth. Open your mouth and your heart will open as well. Speak the Name and discover who you truly are.

Rabbi Rami Shapiro is an award-winning author, poet, essayist, and educator whose poems have been anthologized in over a dozen volumes, and whose prayers are used in prayer books around the world. Rami received rabbinical ordination from the Hebrew Union College–Jewish Institute of Religion and holds doctoral degrees in both Jewish studies and divinity. A congregational rabbi for 20 years, Rabbi Shapiro currently teaches Religious Studies at Middle Tennessee State University, and directs One River (**www.one-river.org**), a not-for-profit educational foundation devoted to building community through contemplative conversation. Rami writes a regular column for Spirituality and Health Magazine called Roadside Assistance on Your Spiritual Journey. His most recent books are The Sacred Art of Lovingkindness, The Divine Feminine, and Open Secrets from which this essay was adapted. Rabbi Rami can be reached through his website, **www.rabbirami.com**

◆ SWAMI BHUTESHANANDA

≈ REALIZING OUR TRUE NATURE ≈
A Simple Answer to the Question, "Who Am I?"

This article is based upon a talk given by the revered Swami Bhuteshanandaji Maharaj at the Sri Ramakrishna Ashrama, Jalpaiguri, on 22 March, 1990. We offer our gratitude to The Udbodan for granting permission to print it in this issue of *Nectar*.

When asked to discuss the real nature of God, I sometimes think: What do we really know about God on the basis of which we can think about His nature? Arjuna says to Sri Krishna in the *Gita* (10.15): *"You alone know Yourself through Yourself, O Supreme Person!"* Nobody but God knows Himself. But if a devotee can merge himself completely in God, can lose his identity in Him, then he may know what God is really like. But then that devotee would have become God. Because when his individuality is completely merged in God, he will acquire the nature of God.

When we try to understand the nature of God in our present state, what are we really doing? We are trying to understand the infinite by the means of our finite minds. This desire to know the infinite is ingrained us, because in reality our finitude is imaginary. It is said in the *Shvetashvatara Upanishad* (5.9): *"Know the embodied soul to be a part of the hundredth part of a point of a hair divided a hundred times, and yet it is infinite."* How can the individual soul become infinite? By merging completely in God.

A wave rises in the infinite ocean, and for some time it seems that it has an identity of its own. But after a while it merges in the ocean and loses its separate identity. All the different objects of this universe are waves in the infinite *Brahman*, the Ultimate Reality. As the Master [Sri Ramakrishna] says, *"God is like an ocean, and living beings are its bubbles. They are born there and they die there."* (Gospel, p. 788) In reality, the bubbles don't exist apart from the ocean, and they can't retain their separate form for long. Now, for people like us, trying to know God is like a bubble trying to measure the ocean. But it should also be remembered that, in reality, the bubble is not different from the ocean.

The scriptures tell us that the whole universe has emanated from one Reality. The universe contains innumerable beings. It may be possible to count the number of sand particles on a beach, but it is impossible to count the number of living beings in the universe. How tiny we are! But we don't want to remain tiny. Even a small child wants to grow up as soon as possible. He doesn't like his own shoes, and wants to wear the shoes of his father. We don't want to remain bound by this earth, and want to travel in space.

Where this quest for expanding our horizons in the external world will lead to, no one knows. But the sum and substance is that we don't want to remain stuck in one place and always want to advance in every way. This feeling of wanting to expand is deeply rooted in our nature, because actually we are that infinite Reality. Something within is always telling us that we are not tiny and insignificant creatures. Although it may not be equally obvious to each person, each one of us — learned or ignorant — is hearing that call, and it is not possible to ignore it forever. Until we succeed in immersing our limitations in the infinite, we will remain restless.

The problem is that we don't know how to overcome our limitations. We are like the frog in a well which jumps around only in the small area the well occupies. Who can help us? We are trapped in the merry-go-round of this world and are suffering in consequence. What is the way out? The Master says: *"You won't have to play the part of the thief again in the game of hide-and-seek once you touch the granny."* (Gospel, p. 714) (F.N. The allusion is to the Indian game of hide-and-seek, in which the leader, known as the "granny," blindfolds the eyes of the players and hides herself. The players are supposed to find her. If any player can touch her, the blindfold is removed from his eyes and he is released from the game.) If someone becomes very tired by his efforts to touch the "granny," the "granny," out of compassion, reaches out her hand so that he can touch her. God is waiting to reach out His hand to us. He is waiting for us to have the required longing.

Incarnations of God can be compared to the "granny." They come to arouse our spiritual consciousness, to awaken us from our slumber. They stand before us and say: *"Arise and awake! Don't lie down on the path. You are not a helpless creature. Realize your real nature!"* Swamiji's parable of the "sheep-lion" may be mentioned in this context. A lion cub thought himself to be a sheep. To dehypnotize him, a full-grown lion took him to the water and made him see his reflection. He also gave him meat to eat. Seeing what he looked like and tasting the meat, the cub realized his true nature.

When we fail to get rid of our limitations by our own efforts, then an incarnation takes hold of us and reveals to us our real nature by degrees. If he did it all at once, we wouldn't be able to bear it. We would become afraid and begin bleating, like the sheep in Swamiji's story. That is why the incarnation does this by degrees. When the Lord showed his universal form to Arjuna, even a mighty warrior like Arjuna began to tremble in fright, because he saw how insignificant he was before God. We have to realize that in reality we are not different from God, and this will only be possible if God makes us understand it by degrees.

That is why God incarnates Himself as a human being. When He assumes a human form, He behaves exactly like a human being, experiencing hunger, thirst, old age, disease, and the like. He mixes with devotees and reveals His real nature to them by degrees. God is ever present in our hearts, but unfortunately we don't seek Him there. For this we will have to turn our minds inwards, which we don't want to do. That is why, like the full-grown lion in Swamiji's story, God comes to us, opens our eyes, and tells us, *"You are what I am!"* But even then some peo-

> "I often hear parents telling their spiritually inclined young boys: "Why this craze for practising spirituality at this young age? Do all that when you grow old." But those parents themselves have become old! Are they directing their minds towards God? They are still doing what they have been doing all their lives, which is running after worldly objects."

ple don't believe Him. As the Lord says in the *Gita* (9.11): *"Fools disregard Me when I assume a human form; for they are unaware of My higher nature as the Supreme Lord of all beings."*

Many people used to deride the Master and make fun of him. But the Master didn't mind all that. He cheerfully accepted the sufferings which ordinary human beings are subject to. And what great efforts he made to reveal to us our divine nature! To his disciple, Niranjan, he once said with great earnestness: *"My boy, the days are passing; when will you realize God? And if you do not realize God, your whole life will be meaningless. I am extremely anxious as to when you will wholeheartedly devote yourself to God."* Why was the Master so anxious? Because he knew that once he had gone, it wouldn't be so easy for Niranjan to realize God, so a great opportunity would be lost. He is waiting to give us his invaluable treasures, but who wants to accept them?

His call is eternal. Those who have been awakened, whose hearts have been purified to some extent, will be able to hear this call. And when they hear it, they realize how insignificant worldly concerns are. A song runs thus: *"Listen! The Lord of my heart is calling, and I have to go!"* God resides in our hearts, and is calling us from there. We sometimes hear this call, but fail to find its source. We are constantly searching for Him outside. We search for him in various centers of pilgrimage and build temples for Him to stay in. But we don't understand that He is actually the Soul of our soul. According to the *Kena Upanishad* (1.2), *"It [Brahman] is the Ear of the ear, the Mind of the mind, the Speech of speech, the Life of life, and the Eye of the eye."* It is the power behind the sense-organs. Then how can It be known? That is why God incarnates Himself, to enable us to know Him.

Coming in the midst of us in human form, He says, *"Know my true nature."* On knowing Him, nothing remains to be known. But not everyone who has had the good fortune to come in contact with an incarnation is able to understand his true nature. As mentioned before, many deride him, thinking him to be an ordinary human being. Most of them don't even get a chance to hear his words. Even when they do, not many are able to understand his teachings. And even among those who understand, very few are able to know His true nature.

Why does this happen? Because we don't have the real yearning which will enable us to know God. The Master has repeatedly stressed in the Gospel that we can't realize God without possessing the requisite yearning. How to get that yearning? We will have to unify all the desires we have for acquiring the different objects of the world, and then direct them towards God. As the Master says, *"The point is, to love God even as the mother loves her child, the chaste wife her husband, and the worldly man his wealth. Add together these three forces of love, these three powers of attraction, and give it all to God. Then you will certainly see Him."* (Gospel, p. 83) The Master used these examples because all of us are familiar with the nature of these three attractions. Otherwise, the yearning for God is such that it can't really be described.

We can't make progress until we have yearning. Should we sit doing nothing and wait for yearning to possess us? No; yearning for God will arise only as a result of our efforts to direct our mind towards God. We perform spiritual practices as a matter of routine. We repeat the name of God a certain number of times only because our gurus have told us to do so. But we are not aware of where our mind goes while we are doing this. We are in a stupor. We should ask ourselves what we are really doing.

I often hear parents telling their spiritually inclined young boys: *"Why this craze for practising spirituality at this young age? Do all that when you grow old."* But those parents themselves have become old! Are they directing their minds towards God? They are still doing what they have been doing all their lives, which is running after worldly objects.

The Master has assured us that even if a room has been kept dark for a thousand years, the moment a light is brought into it, the darkness instantly vanishes. (Gospel, p. 298) When God showers His grace, all the darkness of our minds will vanish in an instant. But for this we shall have to keep the doors and windows of our minds open. Otherwise, God's light will not enter inside. There is light all around us, but we keep our eyes closed. Opening our eyes means to practise spiritual disciplines like prayer and meditation. According to the Master, these are the means to purify our minds. As the mind becomes purified, we slowly develop a real attraction for God; and then only, by His grace, can we earnestly strive to attain Him.

Let us pray to Him to awaken our spiritual consciousness, as does the *Isha Upanishad* (15): *"The door of the Truth is covered by a golden disc. O Lord, remove it so that I who have been worshipping the Truth may behold it."* This much is sure: if we pray to God earnestly, He is bound to listen.

Swami Bhuteshananda, born on 8 September, 1901, was the 12th President of the Ramakrishna Order. In 1921 Saradananda initiated Vijay with Mantradiksha at the Mother's house. He was bestowed the vows of Brahmacharya by Shivananda in 1923 on Holy Mother's birthday. He was thereafter appointed the president of the Ramakrishna Math in Shillong, and of the Rajkot Math in 1945, and became one of the Trustees of the Governing body of the Ramakrishna Mission. In 1975 he became one of the Vice-Presidents of the Order and moved over to Kankurgachi Yogodyan. During his twenty-three years as Vice President and President of the Order he travelled to Singapore, Fiji, Japan, Australia, America, Canada, England, France, Bangladesh, and Sri Lanka, carrying the ideals and ideas of Ramakrishna-Mother-Vivekananda to innumerable people. He passed on in 1998.

Wisdom Facets From the Gem of Truth

Sri Ramakrishna

Siva Sahasrara Meditation.

"If a man is able to weep for God, he will see Him. He will go into samadhi. Perfection in Yoga is samadhi. A man achieves kumbhaka without any yogic exercise if he but weeps for God. There is another method as well — that of meditation. In the Sahasrara, Siva manifests Himself in a special manner. The aspirant should meditate on Him. The body is like a tray, the body and mind are like water. The sun of Satchitananda is reflected in this water. Meditating on this reflected sun, one sees the Real Sun through the Grace of God."

(Gospel of Sri Ramakrishna)

The Slate of the Mind wiped Clean....

"There are two kinds of meditation, one on the formless God and the other on God with form. But meditation on the formless God is extremely difficult. In that meditation you must wipe out all that you see and hear. You contemplate only the nature of your Inner Self."

(Gospel of Sri Ramakrishna)

Oblivious to Senses and Serpents

"A man can achieve such single-mindedness in meditation that he will see nothing, hear nothing. He will not be conscious even of touch. A snake may crawl over his body, but he will not know it; neither of them will be aware of the other. One sign of true meditation is that a bird will sit on the top of a man's head, thinking him to be an inert thing."

(Gospel of Sri Ramakrishna)

How the Jnani Meditates

"Do you know how a jnani meditates? Everywhere is water; all the regions above and below are filled with water; man, like a fish, is swimming joyously in that water. In real meditation you will actually see this. Do you know another way the jnani meditates? Think of infinite akasha and a bird flying there, joyfully spreading its wings. There is the Chidakasha, and Atman is the bird. The bird is not imprisoned in a cage; it flies in the Chidakasha. Its joy is limitless."

(Gospel of Sri Ramakrishna)

Holy Mother, Sri Sarada Devi

The Name of the Avatar, and Meditation

"Most obstacles to worship are not external; they are internal. They will gradually fall off one after another by taking the Master's name and by meditation. Do your duty and keep the mind on God. Don't pay attention to whether the blemishes of the mind are persisting or not, for we are behind you. You all have come to me because you are all my own. If one is the 'very own' of another, they remain inseparably connected in successive cycles of time. I have indeed taken your responsibility."

(Sri Sarada Vijnanagita)

"Oh Mother, What do you see in Your Meditations"

For the welfare of Her devotees She would spend Her nights in japa and meditation. On their behalf She would maker japa of those Great Mantras that She had imparted to them. Along with this She would meditate on Her disciple's and devotee's effulgent Real Nature, which is eternally related to, and united with, the chosen deities eventually to be realized through their respective mantras. How, otherwise, would the devotees be able to discover their obscure Real Nature unless it was revealed to the Mother in Her own meditation?

(Excerpt from The Compassionate Mother)

Preceptor, Practice, and Meditation

"One should practice self-control after the birth of one or two children. And such a one may also give up the world after making provisions for one's dependents. So perform japa with love, sincerity, and self-surrender. Then meditate upon the Lord. Remember how helpless you are in this world and slowly begin sadhana as directed by your Guru."

(Sri Sarada Vijnanagita)

Ready or Not, Here They Come!

"There should be a regular time for japa and meditation, for no one knows when the auspicious moment will come. It comes suddenly; one has no hint of it beforehand. Therefore, regularity in meditation should be observed."

(Sri Sarada Vijnanagita)

Wisdom Facets From the Gem of Truth

Painting by Swami Tadatmananda

Swami Vivekananda

"Meditate Upon the Lord as Thine Own Self,...."

"He who has hidden Himself inside the atom, this Ancient One resides within the inmost recess of every human heart. The sages realized Him through the power of meditation, and got beyond both joy and misery, beyond what we call virtue and vice, beyond good and bad deeds, beyond being and nonbeing; the one who has seen Him has seen the Reality." (Swami Vivekananda, Jnana Yoga)

Get Your Violent Tendencies Under Control

"The meat-eating animal, like the lion, gives one blow and then subsides, but the patient bullock goes on all day, eating and sleeping as it walks. The 'live Yankee' cannot compete with the rice-eating Chinese coolie. While military power dominates, meat-eating will prevail; but with the advance of science, fighting will grow less, and then the vegetarian will come in." (Swami Vivekananda, Inspired Talks)

The Supremacy of Prema, Love

"When you serve an embodied soul with the idea that he is a jiva, it is daya, compassion, and not prema, love; but when you serve him with the idea that he is the Self, that is prema. That the Atman is the one objective of love is known from shruti, smriti, and anubhava. Bhagavan Chaitanya was right when He said: "Love to God, compassion to the jiva." This conclusion of the Bhagavan, intimating differentiation between Jiva and Ishvara was right, as He was a dualist. But for us, Advaitans, this notion of jiva as distinct from God is the cause of bondage. Our principle should be, therefore, love and not compassion. The application of the word compassion even to jivas seems to me to be rash and vain. For us, it is not to pity, but to serve. Ours is not the feeling of compassion but of love, and the feeling of Self in all."
 (Swami Vivekananda, Swami Vivekananda Vijnanagita)

Manahpranasambandah – Connecting Senses to Mind

"Unless we join the mind with the senses, we get no real report from eyes, nose, ears. The external senses are used by the power of the mind." (Swami Vivekananda, Inspired Talks)

Disciples & Devotees of Sri Ramakrishna

Beyond Real and Unreal

"The Vedas proclaim, 'Ekamevadvitiyam — That is One; nothing exists apart from that Brahman.' Truth is one and indivisible. If you count the world as true and real, Brahman comes to be meaningless and nonexistent. On the other hand, if you look upon Brahman as true, the world comes to be without meaning or substance. Both the world and Brahman cannot be true at the same time if they are one and the same thing. When we say that the world is an illusion and Brahman alone constitutes the Truth, we mean that what appears to be the world is actually a manifestation of Brahman." (Swami Abedhananda, Journey into Kashmir & Tibet)

Christ and Krishna, Bible and Brahman

"Christ taught us to seek God within. In the Gospel of Luke we read: 'The kingdom of God cometh not with observation: neither shall they say, Lo here! or, Lo there!, for behold, the kingdom of God is within you.' When the mind has been purified through spiritual disciplines and is able to turn inward upon itself, man realizes that his true being is Atman-Brahman. To uncover this true Being, or Divinity, which lies hidden within oneself, is to become perfect. This is the technique of all spiritual practice." (Swami Prabhavananda, The Sermon On The Mount According to Vedanta)

Tit for Tat, this for That

"Whenever the world is thwarted and saddened, it looks for a new vision; but when all goes well, it settles back into the old way again. It is natural to turn to God when we are forsaken by men and misunderstood by friends and family; but we do not truly worship Him until we come seeking nothing of Him. We must outgrow the habit of bargaining, of asking a fair return in personal benefit for our service to God. That attribute always limits our ability to express the Divine."
 (Swami Paramananda, Christ and the Oriental Ideal)

Scriptural Sayings
of the World's Religious Traditions

"As in a house with a sound roof the rain cannot penetrate, just so, in a mind where meditation dwells, passion cannot enter and disturb. Those who control the mind in meditation, which otherwise wanders afar, solitary, incorporeal, and which resides in the cavern of the heart, will liberate themselves from the shackles of Mara and transcend rebirth."

"Without meditation there is no tranquility, and without tranquility how shall there be lasting happiness? The mind that orders itself according to the motions of the senses, carries away the intelligence as the wind carries away a ship on the breast of the sea. Therefore, only he whose senses are drawn back from the objects of the senses has a firmly seated wisdom."

"How can he remain long in peace who troubles himself with foreign cares and worries, who seeks to diffuse himself into the outward only, and who withdraws, little by little, or rarely, into himself? If a man possess the true Light within him, darkness cannot lodge in his soul. Who can describe the peace of that luminous country where the true Light shines out forever in its limpid purity?"

"He who meditates upon righteousness and mercy, findeth life and honor. For if a man does what is lawful and right, and does not oppress any, but has restored to the debtor his pledge, has spoiled none by violence, hath given bread to the hungry and has covered the naked with a garment – he who has not given forth upon usury, neither has taken any increase, he is just."

"The present world and the next are but a drop of water whose existence is of no lasting account. Since the world passes, do thou thyself pass beyond it. The one who does shall contemplate under the veil millions of secrets as radiant as the sun."

"Whoever applies himself intelligently to profound meditation, soon finds peace and joy in what is good. He thinks actively, he opens his heart, and he gathers up all of his inner illuminations. He becomes conscious that things such as beauty and riches are transient, and that wisdom is by far the fairest of all ornaments."

BABAJI BOB KINDLER

EYES OPEN, EYES CLOSED
Meditation as Presence Rather Than Practice

Holy Mother, Sri Sarada Devi, has coined the perfect statement in regards to meditation. Speaking to Her precious spiritual children about the subject, She uttered: *"Does God (Brahman) exist only when eyes are closed, and cease to exist when eyes are open?"* Following up on this revealing point, She stated: *"Please do not just seek God; see God."* The subtle problem is this: the act of meditation, itself, causes a rift in our otherwise indivisible and homogenous Awareness.

The Avadhut Speaks

The all-pervasive Soul — *Atman* — is God; there is no other God in existence. This God is our own Self, or our Essence — *svarupa*. As long as the apparent soul, the transmigrating body/mind mechanism, wanders the three worlds (outside, inside, beyond; gross, subtle, causal; earth, heaven, higher heaven; waking, dreaming, deep sleep; *bhur, bhuvah, svaha, A, U, M*, etc.), just so long will the spiritually oriented acts of concentration and meditation accent divisiveness in the soul. Yet, when these various *triputis* are connected — that is, are realized to be intrinsically enwrapped within divinely realized human Consciousness — meditation is, of a sudden, both natural and spontaneous, occurring at all times, beyond time, and transcendent of space. In disbelief at all that is blind, dull, and dim in human awareness, the Avadhut adamantly declares in his *Gita*:

> *"There is no separate space, inside or out, in Atman.
> So how can there be a place to meditate
> or a meditator striving to go within?
> No form can be where no space exists,
> so who is it that you are trying so hard to see?
> Samadhi is simply your true Nature.
> You are Pure Existence, Wisdom, and Bliss Absolute,
> as boundless as the sky, infinite like space."*

Pippalada, the ancient *rishi* of India, teaches the art of spiritual connections in the *Upanisads*. He avers that, *"The ignorant soul imagines the three lower nadis to be separate, and thus wanders in bondage. The aware soul, getting wisdom from the Vedanta, does not suffer delusion from the three lowers states (waking, dreaming, and deep sleep), realizing the oneness (with Turiya) of all four of them."*

To connect the waking state, A, with the dreaming state, U, into the deep sleep state, M, is to become a knower of The Word — AUM. To a knower of The Word, meditation is always deep, ever accompanied by the cohesive wisdom-power of *Shakti*. States the *Para-Brahma Upanisad*, *"This sacred, secret lore of Nondual Wisdom shines brilliantly in the resplendent city of the Transcendent Brahman. Like a hive of intoxicated bees, illumined souls meditate naturally in the Divine Ether of Brahman's Heart, long before any inception."* "Before any inception" indicates the unoriginated nature of Consciousness. If there is any other prime subject of meditation for the lover of *Brahman* who is in constant communion with That, the unoriginated nature of Existence would be it. And what of matter? Matter proves no problem here. Matter is only a problem if one considers it to be real — what to speak of the only reality. As my guru, Swami Aseshanandaji Maharaj, has stated: *"Western Science believes matter to be real, and destructible. It is not destructible, nor is it indestructible; it is unoriginated."*

And outstripping matter, what about that which created (projected) matter. Most beings in contemporary times (*Kali Yuga*) do not know that matter proceeds from thought; nature only provides the gross and subtle elements (*tattvas*) for that transition. To detach and get beyond matter, then, would require eliminating the thinking process, or at least purifying it. Thus, mind and ego would have to be subjected to the *sattvic* and *tattvic* melting pot of intense concentration. A peaceful inner scrutiny of all that the mind produces in the realm of thought will therefore have to be undergone. After intense exposure to such a process, the Avadhut comes forth to say,

> *"The creation of the many worlds was not for our benefit; Brahman is beyond them, and we are That.
> It is the shameful ego/mind that has vomited them out.
> Unity with diversity is not for us, is not our Nature.
> We are Pure Existence, Wisdom, and Bliss,
> as boundless as the sky, infinite like space."*

Given that meditating upon one's sole Essence is difficult, unattracting, and not possible for most embodied souls, the seers recommend a regimen of intense *sadhana* that will direct the mind's consciousness back towards its original nondual state. As has already been mentioned, most human beings are both disinterested in religion and spiritual life, and react with apathy even if they do hear of it or come across it.

This is reminiscent of the ancient story in the sacred scripture, *Yoga Vasishtha*, of Lord Brahma sending his mind-born son, Vasishtha, to earth, *Bhur-loka*, from *Brahma-loka*. First, the Lord put him in a *mayic* spell wherein Vasishtha reeled in confusion and suffering. Next, he brought him out of it to ask him what the experience had been like for him (this question, "How did you feel about that," has been around for some time, it seems).

His son described for him the completely disoriented and tormented state of mind he had just been exposed to, and asked his father why he had taken away his usually balanced state of peace of mind in such a fashion. Lord Brahma replied, *"It is because you are going to have to take a body soon on Bhur Loka (Earth) in order to help many bound souls there gain freedom, and I wanted you to actually know what they feel like in their presently stunted condition. You will have more empathy with them as a result."*

Lord Brahma went on to advise his son that he would meet five types of souls on Earth, and told him: *"The evil ones will hate and revile you, so remain aloof from them. The worldly souls will have no interest in what you teach at all, so do not waste your time with them. Most of the suffering beings on earth prefer their habitual forms of pain and pleasure to the type of suffering that awakens the soul from ignorance; do what you can for them but remember their penchant for rebirth in ignorance. Very few of them really want to awaken"*

"The other two types of souls should be your focus," the Lord went on to say. *"There are illumined souls on Earth doing selfless service to God in mankind. Seek them out for holy company, but know that they do not need what you will be teaching. It is the fifth type of soul that you should seek out and attract. These are the ones who have or are sincerely seeking the spiritual qualifications called, "The Four Treasures and the Six Jewels."* [see Nectar issue #29, "Vedanta and Today's Youth," for chart and teachings on the Four Treasures] *To these you should give your full attention, helping them to perfect themselves on earth and transcend it forthwith. Fear not! The world-bewitching maya will not inhibit or impede you"*

Empty Sandwich:
White Bread; Nothing in the Middle

The stark problem in today's interested souls, few as they are, is having access to only two strata of available spirituality: first, the sunken grounds of physical practices like hatha, food-faddism, new age psychology, and beginning exercises such as these; or, on the opposite spectrum, introduction into high-minded, advanced philosophies such as Advaita Vedanta, Zen, and other schools of Buddhism. This latter level is where meditation gets practiced in earnest. The former strata are interested only in physical health, pleasures, prana, and living a pseudo-spiritual existence devoid of austerities and real spiritual growth.

Taking up these two (beginning and elevated) levels of practice in today's emerging spirituality for observation, it seems to be a sandwich with no filling — like two pieces of white bread devoid of any healthy middle parts. Where is the fat, nutty Hawaiian avocado of devotional worship? Where is the delicious, juicy tomato of timeless cosmology? Where have the crisp lettuce of scriptural study and the organic alfalfa sprouts of deep contemplation gone to, what to speak of the eggy, oleaginous mayonnaise of meditation upon divine forms who lead and guide the soul to mature, formless realization? Sprinkle in the toasted sunflower seeds of selfless works for humanity and replace the two pieces of nutritionless white bread with the two, whole grain bread slices of desire for Enlightenment and Service of God in mankind, and the soul starts to live again. It is to be noticed that this savory sandwich is vegetarian so that no violence is committed upon our animal friends as well. As Vivekananda has stated, *"While military power dominates, meat-eating will prevail; but with the advance of science and religion, fighting will grow less, and then the vegetarian will come in."*

The New Religion of this Age

Swamiji has made the astute declaration that the new religion of this age is the combined Four Yogas [see chart on facing page]. He brought them back to earth in this age and had four books of his talks on them published in America. The one on *Raja Yoga*, which is the traditional path of meditation in India as put forth by Patanjali in his Eight-Limbed Yoga, is a purposefully simple commentary meant to interest Westerners in this profound path. Unfortunately, the awakening few are rushing towards *hatha yoga* only which, on its own, is worthless for Enlightenment. These beings are also interested in the show and spectacle that proceeds from the occult side of this yoga, though it is dangerous for both life and the pursuit of spiritual realization. With practical intelligence, and a guide such as him, these various dangers can be surmounted.

The *Jnana Yoga* is also key to meditation. As the analogy of the sandwich has inferred, inner substance that lies on the upper part of the filling — the part that lies up against the upper slice of bread — is contemplation on the wisdom scriptures as transmitted by the spiritual preceptor. Vacant minds, thinking themselves to be in meditation, are truly "empty" if there is no inspiration coming from hearing the truth of the dharma from the lips of an illumined soul. Great thoughts, powerful words — these are the twin springboards to vault the high-minded seeker into actual meditation. Hearing, pondering, and realizing have always been the three proofs of the proof of Brahman in India [see article on page 10 of this issue]

> "Vacant minds, thinking themselves to be in meditation, are truly "empty" if there is no inspiration coming from hearing the truth of the dharma from the lips of an illumined soul. Great thoughts, powerful words — these are the twin springboards to vault the high-minded seeker into actual meditation. In addition, by utilizing the *bhakti* elements of worship, and meditating on God with form, the mind will never get lost in abstruse atmospheres of unknowing ever again."

In addition, by utilizing the *bhakti* elements of worship, and meditating on God with form, the mind will never get lost in abstruse atmospheres of unknowing again. *Samadhi* — which is the summation of all meditation practice — will come, and whereas the lower wisdom samadhis are not so uncommon to advanced practitioners, the nondual Samadhi that we saw in Sri Ramakrishna Paramahamsa, Ramana Maharshi, and Swami Vivekananda, are not coming westward. Why would they, when there is no tasty filling in the Samadhi sandwich here.

The Four Yogas and Their Synthesis

Bhakti Yoga — *Union with Reality via One-pointed Devotion*

Raja Yoga — *Union with Reality via Focused Meditation on Divine Reality*

The Four Yogas Defined

Jnana Yoga — *Union with Reality via Knowledge of the Atman*

Karma Yoga — *Union with Reality via Selfless Action offered as Service to God in Mankind*

"The teaching of the new Incarnation, Sri Ramakrishna, is that the best points of Yoga, Devotion, Knowledge, and Work must be combined so as to form a new society." — Swami Vivekananda

Bhakti – Yoga of Devotion to God

"Serene-minded, beyond both grief and desire, same-sighted and kind to all, such a one attains supreme devotion to Me."

- Listen to Accounts of God's Deeds
- Engage Sincerely in Devotional Rituals
- Purify Heart and Mind via Daily Worship
- Sing Praises to the Lord and Mother
- Get Initiation into the Spiritual Path
- Perform Japa of the Holy Names
- Engage Earnestly in Meditative Prayer
- Increase Devotion to Ishvara

Jnana – Yoga of Discerning Wisdom

"He whose intellect is unattached everywhere, who is endowed with nondual understanding, that one reaches consummate Knowledge."

- Recite the Slokas of the Scriptures
- Memorize the Slokas of the Scriptures
- Take Teachings from an Illumined Teacher
- Comprehend the Meaning of the Scriptures
- Discriminate between the Real and Unreal
- Penetrate through the Cosmic Appearance
- Contemplate the Nature of Reality
- Abide Continually in Nondual Realization

"I want to give Truth dry hard reason, softened in the sweetest syrup of love, and made spicy with intense work, and cooked in the kitchen of Yoga so that even a baby can easily digest it." — Swami Vivekananda

Raja – Yoga of Meditation/Samadhi

"Dwell in solitude, restrain the senses, control the mind, and engage in meditation. You will thus reach perfection in Brahman."

- Calm and Control the Mind's Thoughts
- Purge the Mind of Desire and Passions
- Still the Mind's Tendency of Distraction
- Uncover and Neutralize all Karmas
- Dissolve the Mind's Limiting Impressions
- Reach the Samadhi of Wisdom
- Gain Kaivalya — Isolation from Nature
- Immerse into Nirvikalpa Samadhi

Karma – Yoga of Selfless Action

"Performing actions selflessly and continually while taking refuge in Me, by My grace he reaches the eternal, undecaying Abode."

- Engage Only in Obligatory Actions
- Renounce Action done for Selfish Motive
- Perform all Action with Evenness of Mind
- Do not Seek the Fruits of Action
- Detach from all the Outcomes of Action
- Perform all Work as Worship
- Utilize all Work to Serve God in Mankind
- Work Meticulously but with Detachment

"Would to God that all men were so constituted that in their minds all of these elements — philosophy, mysticism, emotion, and work — were equally present in full! That is the ideal, my ideal of a perfect man. Everyone who has only one or two of these elements I consider one-sided; and this world is almost full of such 'one-sided' men, with knowledge of that one road only in which they move." — Vivekananda

I Said Cosmology, Not Cosmetology

The mention of an ancient, well-matured cosmology has been made earlier, an intelligent way inwards — like a trail of breadcrumbs through the forest of *maya* — by which the embodied soul can consciously trace his or her way back to the Source of origin. For those who do not count the body as real, or even that important in life (even the celestial bodies, angelic bodies, and godly bodies), of the greatest import is to return to the indivisible, eternal state of Formlessness after sporting and serving God in mankind in the body, on earth, is over. Other than the primordial systems followed by the Native Americans, whom those of European descent rejected and tried to wipe off of the face of this earth, America has no such cosmological philosophy to follow, inwardly. The gods and goddesses of Greece and Rome were short-lived, indeed — in Greece, Italy, and America. Just as in Jesus's time, the West has almost no grasp on inner life, i.e., eternal life; their lives are lived externally only.

But Americans delight in painting themselves up with makeup and pretending that they are gods and goddesses, and being other than who they truly are. This lower urge was looked upon as an occult power in ancient India, and looked askance at by the luminaries. Imagine the jaw-dropping, open mouthed, utter surprise of beings like Swami Vivekananda when he arrived here in 1893 to see such "fair faces with false hearts" parading about in vain fashion. To quote him:

"To the people of the West, ministering to the body is a great thing: they would trim and polish and give their whole attention to that. A thousand instruments for paring nails, ten thousand for haircutting, and who can count the varieties of dress and toilet and perfumery. They are a thoroughly materialistic country. It will take a long time for them to understand spirituality…."

Taking note of the state of things here, it did not take the swami much time to begin shipping over spiritual books from India to America, and having his brother monks bring them over as well. It is due to him, and to the Order that He founded in his Guru's name, that America benefits by what knowledge of Sanskrit, Eastern Cosmology, Philosophy, and Spirituality that it has today. Vedanta and Yoga were the first for him to teach, and along with them came the initial books of authentic cosmology (*Sankhya*) and real worship (*Tantra*). He gave us the heart of India [see chart on facing page]. Now we must use what he gifted us to gain Enlightenment — freedom from the limitations of nature, the sporadic tendencies of the immature mind/ego complex, and the difficult to avoid clutches of *maya*.

Karmas Cling to Tattvas

One of the advantages of Cosmology is that it outlines the order and the meanings of things in time. This is called *kala* and *kalas* in Sanskrit. Finding out that time is a concept created in the mind proves a boon to seekers of freedom. Lord Buddha indicated this by his teachings on swimming out of the river and sitting on the banks for awhile, observing. It is only then that one can see everything moving in circular fashion in endless cycles (*kalas*), and thus develop the desire to be free from them.

But another facet of the presence of a well-defined cosmology, lesser known to seekers of Truth, is that the location of *karmas* can be pinpointed thereby. Seekers suffer their karmas well into advanced phases of their spiritual practice simply because they do not know where to look for them, i.e., to find where they are lodged and ferret them out. Thus, their progress along the path is hampered overall, and what is more, the awful danger of quitting the path becomes more likely.

To come to know about and study the five elements (*bhutas*), the fives senses (*karmendriyas*), the subtle elements (*tanmatras*), the subtle senses (*jnanendriyas*), and their connections to the mind/ego complex (*antahkarana*) — all facets (*tattvas*) of *Sankhya* Cosmology — is to come (or stumble) upon the heretofore hidden presence of residues of actions perpetrated in the past, both in this present life, and in the previous ones.

These residues (*karmashaya*), that later form nearly immovable mental impressions (*samskaras*) in the human mind, cling to the *tattvas* (24/36 cosmic principles). They are driven deep into them by ill-considered acts, made to adhere to them due to laziness and complacency (lack of spiritual self-effort), and grow there via the constant fueling of doubt and fear.

> "The beginning aspirant is unable to ascend inwardly because of the presence of unresolved issues occupying the subtle body (inner mind), and the advanced meditator is unable to gain enlightenment and is dragged back to lower levels of awareness for the same reason."

A simple example would be the fear of water due to drowning in a past lifetime. The mind/soul brings that fear composite back into the current life and mind-set, and will not go near water. Only by destroying that fear will the residue dissipate. Just so, *karmas* formed due to thoughts and actions operating in family life, religion, occupation, and all other matters pertinent to relative existence, adhere to the mind at subconscious and unconscious levels, forming the limiting habits, conventions, and lifestyles of individuals — and whole cultures.

This insight into the interdependence of *tattvas* and *karmas*, which is a part of both cosmology and spiritual life combined, reveals that meditation can be seriously hampered by the lack of this knowledge. The beginning aspirant is unable to ascend inwardly because of the presence of unresolved issues occupying the subtle body (inner mind), and the advanced meditator is unable to gain enlightenment and is dragged back to lower levels of awareness for the same reason. This is why the scriptures and the *guru* advise meditation as contemplation, rumination, cogitation (*manana/yukti*) alongside and in conjunction with formal meditation upon Ultimate Reality. This is the method that forms luminaries. It is also, as the poet-saint, Ramprasad, states, *"…the worship and study that disappoints death."*

Mother India's Revealed Scriptures On Earth

> *"The revealed scriptures and spiritual preceptors of the world have their existence through the Atman. Faith, devotion, and constant communion with the wise — these are declared by the scriptures to be the seeker's direct means to realizing It. It is hard for any embodied being to achieve a human form, strength, and purity. More difficult still is the desire to live a spiritual life. And hardest of all is cultivating an ability to comprehend the holy scriptures."* — Shankara

Panchakarana

Hiranyagarbha — Mahat, Buddhi, Ahamkara, Manas, Chitta → 1 — Cosmic Intelligence

Tanmatras — Shabda, Sparsha, Rupa, Rasa, Gandha → 2 — Cosmic Mind / Intellect / Ego / Mind / Thought

Jnanendriyas — Shravenindriya, Sparshendriya, Chakshurindriya, Rasenendriya, Ghranendriya → 3 — Audibility / Tangibility / Visibility / Flavor / Odor

Karmendriyas — Vagendriya, Hastendriya, Padendriya, Upasthendriya, Payuindriya → 4 — Hearing / Feeling / Seeing / Tasting / Smelling

Panchamahabhutas — Vyoma, Marut, Teja, Ap, Kshiti → 5 — Speaking / Handling / Locomotion / Procreating / Excreting — Ether / Air / Fire / Water / Earth

Cosmic Projection

Quintuplication Process

108 Upanisads
Bhagavad Gita
Brahma Sutras

Ashtavakra Samhita
Avadhuta Gita
Srimad Devi Bhagavatam   Adhyatma Ramayana
The Chandi   Gaudapada's Karika

The Four Vedas   Vivekachudamani
The Eighteen Puranas   Aparokshanubhuti
The Sixty-four Tantras   Tattva-Samasa-Sutras   Drg-Drsha-Viveka
The Ramayana   Patanjali's Yoga Sutras Atmabodha
The Mahabharata   Jivan-Mukti-Viveka   Tattvabodha
Srimad Bhagavatam   Panchadasi   Upadesha Sahasri
Uddhava Gita   Dhammapada   Prapancha Sara
Narada's Bhakti Sutras   Yoga Vasishtha   Atma-Anatma-Viveka
Sandilya's Bhakti Sutras   Mohamudgara
The Code of Manu   Vakyavritti

Gospel Of Sri Ramakrishna
Complete Works of Swami Vivekananda

> *"I have never lost faith in a benign Providence, nor am I ever going to lose it. My faith in the true religion and revealed scriptures is unshaken."* — Swami Vivekananda

> "With sweet, one-pointed concentration comes visitations of the Eternal Light,
> perception of the Unstruck Sound of AUM, the descent of Ecstatic Bliss,
> and the vision of Brahman existing everywhere, and in everything."

Concentration *is* True Life

Concentration is life. Put obversely, having a scattered mind is a kind of living death. With sweet, one-pointed concentration comes visitations of the Eternal Light, perception of the Unstruck Sound of *AUM*, the descent of Ecstatic Bliss, and the vision of *Brahman* existing everywhere, and in everything. And what is more, these hosts of blessings seem perfectly natural; they bespeak of the simple and forthright way of things that should be flowing all the while. Meditation is then spontaneous, happening on the spot and in the moment. It is not a practice any longer, but rather a path that one looks back upon as the Hand of God guiding the soul throughout time — for as long as the soul needs or wants time. The Timeless One awaits….waits for the soul to be done with mass, collective mental dreaming. The Ever-Awake state, called "Yogic Insomnia" by Lex Hixon, is then upon the soul.

According to the Father of Yoga, limbs six, seven, and eight of the Yoga Darshana — India's own Triple Gem — occur after mastery over the mind and senses is attained (*pratyahara*). Concentration fuses with meditation, producing experiences of *samadhi* at subtle levels of awareness (*samyama*).

Deifying the Alambanas

Objects are the first to face transformation in consciousness. [see chart on facing page] Whereas prior to mental mastery objects were tripping stones, at this refined stage they are stepping stones. The reason why illumined beings "see Brahman everywhere" is due to the nondual mind's ability to recognize that objects are projections of the mind. If the mind is tending towards the nondual state it sees this process as a clear manifestation of knowledge rather than a product of nature. Seeing this fresh expression outside, then inside, the yogi fuses these two "directions" and experiences *savichara* and *savitarka samadhi* — which is a kind of synthesis between thought and the objects it produces. *Nirvichara* and *nirvitarka* samadhis usually follow, bringing with them the vision of both the disappearance of thoughts and their projected objects — with the observer perfectly aware of this "emptiness," and aware of its state of "Witness Consciousness" as well. The ongoing absence of thoughts and objects produces witness consciousness of the subtle ego and its prized possession of subtle bliss, called *sasmita* and *sananda samadhis* by the Yoga Master, Patanjali. These four *samadhis* are *sabija*, meaning seeded with gross or subtle form.

With regards to meditation per se, this march of inward wisdom *samadhis* is supremely natural. In fact, it is so natural that many very centered beings are only aware that they have had such samadhis years after they have taken place. This is not due to some bright light that occurs to them in practice; it shows itself up in the daily life of a soul who is devout, whose faith is steady, whose mind knows itself, and who is always in meditation — whether eyes are open or shut.

Nirbija: Non-germination

With regards to that rare formless *samadhi*, Sri Ramakrishna Paramahamsa has used the analogy of paddy, or rice seed, that is subjected to flames for just a short time before it is strewn across the land prior to the rainy season. Nothing happens. But if this seed is not subjected to fire before it is spread, an absolute riot of growth will ensue within a short time. In similar fashion, thought-seeds lying deep within the mind, stored at the causal level of awareness, may eventually be watered to produce the riotous growth of worlds in time and space.

Simply put, these seeds lie in the deep sleep state of awareness, and living beings will thereafter, utilizing the water of desire (*sankalpa*), produce thought objects in the dream state. These very thoughts, partaking of the combination of form, sound, vibration, and meaning, as well as the five elements of nature, will solidify and appear in the waking state as tangible worlds and objects. They were all intangible earlier (*tanmatras*); it was the force of thought and intelligence that brought them into manifestation. And in the case of worlds and objects bringing pain, attachment, aversion, and other unsavory elements with them into life, it is the lack of intelligence on the part of the one doing the projecting that is to blame. Thus are all ignoble and unworthy elements of life brought into the picture by incarnating souls, not by god or devil. As Sri Sarada Devi, the Holy Mother, has stated: *"One should never blame God for the sufferings that one experiences."* By the same measure, all the boons and blessings that come into life do not proceed from God either — not the Formless Reality, *Brahman*. "That" (*Tat*) remains ever-pure, transcendent of dualities such as lack and gain.

Nirbija Samadhi — also called *Nirvikalpa, Nirvana, Satori*, etc. — is not just a condition of powerless seeds, or merely of no thoughts. For one thing, it is the outright absence of pain, suffering and ignorance; for another, it is the full on presence of Love, Bliss, and the *"Peace that passeth all understanding."* It is the *"Ocean of Consciousness without Boundaries, the All-Permeating Atmosphere of Utter Sanctity, the Eternal Refuge of the Wise, and the Open Space beyond Religion."* When It does manifest Itself forth in form — as the *Rig Veda* states — it appears as *"The Eternal Companion, The Friend of All Beings, The Living Fire of Yoga, The Waters of Pure Life, The Carrier of Consciousness, The Devourer of Death, and the One Who Shines Forth the Light."*

Babaji Bob Kindler is the Spiritual Director of the SRV Associations with centers in Hawaii, Oregon, and California. A teacher of religion and spirituality and a prolific author, his books include *The Avadhut, Twenty-Four Aspects of Mother Kali, Ten Divine Articles of Sri Durga, Sri Sarada Vijnanagita, Swami Vivekananda Vijnanagita, An Extensive Anthology of Sri Ramakrishna's Stories, A Quintessential Yoga Vasishtha, Reclaiming Kundalini Yoga*, and others. Founder and Artistic Director of Jai Ma Music, he is also an accomplished musician and composer who has produced over twenty-five albums of instrumental and devotional music to date.

The Six Esoteric Yogic Gateways
Yoga's Secret of Transcendence

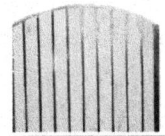 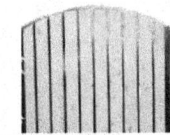

"Each moment arises from Infinity. Each moment dissolves back into Infinity. The next moment also arises directly from Infinity. Concentration upon what is between the dissolution of the prior moment and the arising of the subsequent moment opens the gates of Infinity. These gateways, six in number, are the real powers of an illumined Yogi." — Patanjala Yoga Commentaries

- Perceiving internal movement of particles
- Seeing Time and Space to be apparent
- Observing moments forming the passage of time
- Knowing objects consist of particles
- Knowledge of creation as vibration
- **Comprehension of Eternity**

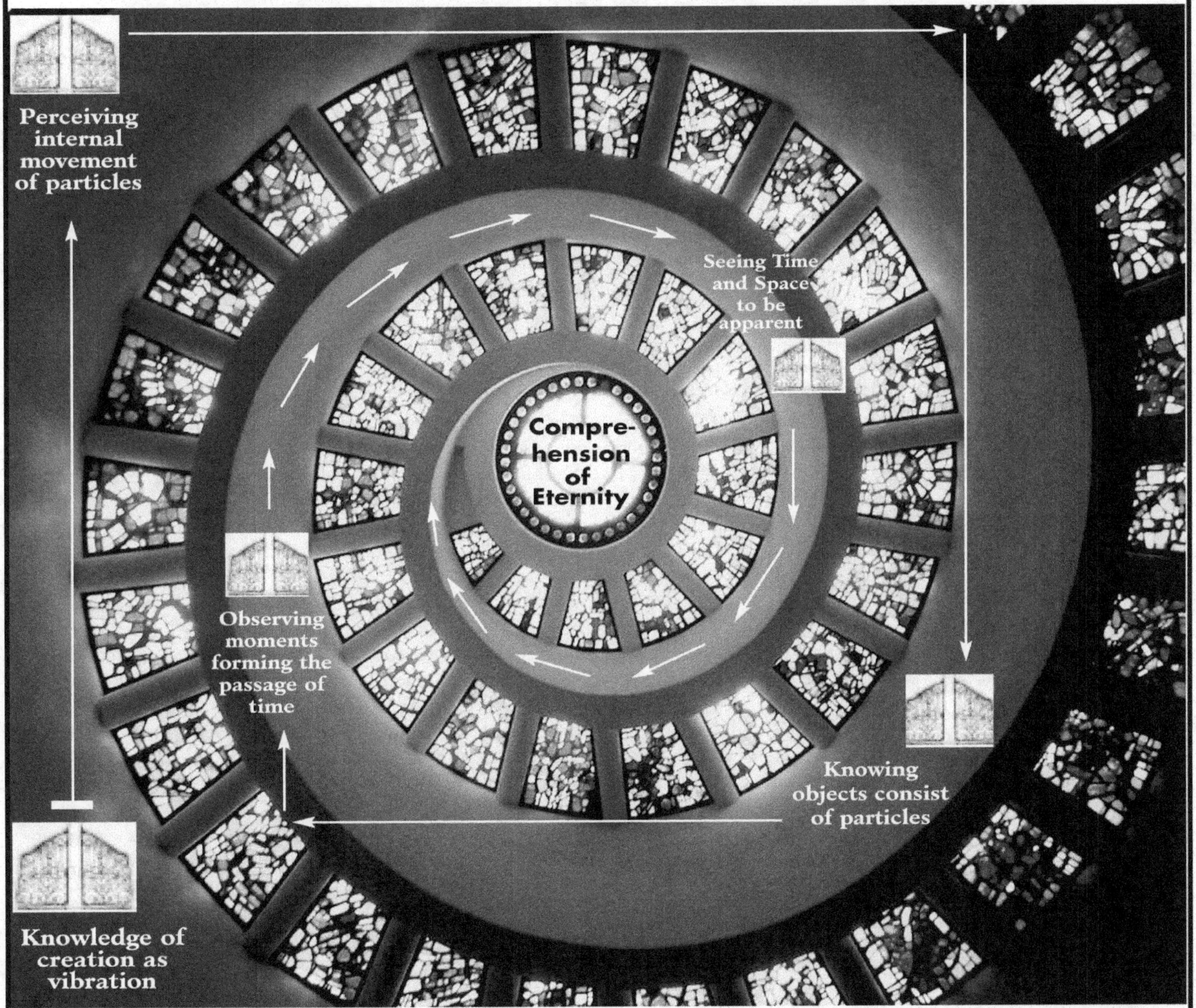

"All of creation is made of vibrating particles. Each particle has an inner movement. Many particles together make up an object. Many moments following one upon another take up time. This cause and effect sequence in time and space is not literal — is only apparent. When this mental notion that time and space are real is transcended, Reality stands forth, revealed." — Patanjala Yoga Commentaries

Chart by Babaji Bob Kindler   Property of SRV Associations

◆ LEX HIXON

SITTING IN CH'AN ZEN RETREAT
A Report on "Who Am I" in Chinese Buddhism

As I write this report, one week has passed since the seven-day retreat with Master Sheng-Yen. This was my first intensive retreat during some fifteen years of daily meditation practice. I was inspired to enter the retreat by a spontaneous confidence in Master Sheng-Yen as a spiritual guide of the highest level. I feel deep karmic connections with him and with the natural, cultural, and spiritual landscape of China, as well as intense attraction to the Truth transmitted by Mahayana Buddhism, particularly by the radical tradition of Ch'an.

I first told Master Sheng-Yen, whom his students call Shih-fu, about coming on this retreat several months ago in a dream when Shih-fu was still in Taiwan. The next morning there was a call from the Ch'an Center, informing me about the exact day of the Master's return to New York City.

Since I have always preferred to meditate peacefully with eyes closed, repeating a mantra mentally with each breath, I began the retreat this way. However, the methodless method of silent illumination which Shih-fu recommended offers no mantra, nor any other particular focus to sustain concentration. This resulted in a rather sleepy, foggy beginning; yet my highly engaged mind began to settle down enough on the second day to receive the kung-an, "Who-am-I?" Shih-fu helped me understand right away that this question had great spiritual power when simply asked for its own sake, again and again, with no expectation for an answer. Any answer which might occur in words should quietly and immediately be put aside. It was my strong confidence in Shih-fu that enabled me to enter wholeheartedly into this process of simply questioning. I experienced faith that this open-ended questioning was imperceptibly sweeping clear the mind and the world. My eyes remained closed, and the mode of my sitting remained peaceful.

On the afternoon of the third day, the question "Who-am-I?" began to stop feeling like a question and became more like a simple statement of fact. It was as if the "Who-am-I?" was my real name, my real identity. There was a quiet surge of inner confidence and joy. I gradually stopped asking the question because it began to feel entirely irrelevant. After the sitting, Shih-fu was immediately aware that something had happened during my meditation and invited me to the interview room. After making the traditional prostration, even before I said anything to him, he told me that I had changed. I felt very happy but not dramatically different. Listening to my report, he explained that I had reached the point where the kung-an disappears. This was a development I had not expected. Perhaps Shih-fu would advise me to pursue the method of silent illumination again, a practice which I could now really engage in authentically. He surprised me by telling me instead to return to the question "Who-am-I?," explaining that I should inquire now with greater intensity as if a wonderful treasure, important to me as life itself, were inside a small box. I should closely examine the box, turning it over and over again, this way and that, to discover how to open it. Once more, it was my confidence in Shih-fu as a spiritual guide that enabled me to set aside my joyous state and plunge back into to the process of radical questioning.

When I returned to the cushion, I found myself sitting in an entirely different mode, not peacefully but with intense determination. My habitually closed eyes were flung wide open and focused with laser-sharp concentration on one minute detail of the wooden wall. Streams of energy seemed to flow from my eyes, as if they were consuming the world. It was impossible to close my eyes or shift my gaze even for an instant. The "Who-am-I?," which I had been repeating peacefully with long breaths, came alive with a power of its own, repeating quickly and decisively like a hammer accurately driving a nail. This continued for several hours until the evening service. I would unfold and refold my legs occasionally, with noticeable interruption of concentration.

This entirely independent life of the kung-an continued about half way through evening chanting and then gradually disappeared. For the whole next day I was unable to reawaken the kung-an through any personal effort. It awakened again spontaneously during dawn meditation, culminating in a thirty-second burst of what Master Sheng-Yen calls Great Angry Determination. The question "Who-am-I?" and I myself became like a single huge red ball of flame. The following sitting passed in deep peace, with a natural mind as free, cool, and refreshing as the early morning breeze that was blowing through the meditation hall.

After breakfast and washing dishes, however, I found once more that the intensity of the "Who-am-I?" could not be recovered by any act of will. Master Sheng-Yen was extremely helpful, asking me to rest my mind and not make futile efforts. The Great Angry Determination did spontaneously return and I meditated instead of going to lunch, not wishing to lose momentum again. The thirty seconds of overwhelming intensity which threatened to shatter me that morning was miraculously sustained for about ten minutes. I felt like a warrior in a life and death battle or like a wrathful Tantric Deity. "I must discover who I am, I absolutely must, not for my own sake but to bring the Truth to all living beings." I roared the kung-an inwardly like a lion, trembling with holy rage in every fiber of my being. Then there was a natural release, and I wept very profoundly. Only once in my life have I wept so deeply, at the funeral of my original meditation teacher, Swami Nikhilananda. The meaning of this extraordinary weeping gradually became conscious: I was a mother and all beings were my children. This was no longer simply a metaphor from the Buddhist sutras, but an actual experience. Great Angry Determination was nothing but infinite compassion and love. Like a wise mother, Shih-fu noted precisely when this powerful experience had resolved itself, leaving me profoundly moved but tired. He asked me to go to the dining hall where my lunch had been carefully saved. Strangely enough, it was vegetable curry, reminding me of the Hindu tradition of the Divine Mother in which I have been practicing for fifteen years.

The Great Angry Determination did not arise again until the last sitting before evening service on the last full day of the retreat. Before, it had come as a flood of unbearable Compassion; now it came as a storm of transcendent Wisdom which utterly devastated, decimated and obliterated not only the entire universe but all Being. Finally, the raging kung-an also eliminated itself. Tears turned to spontaneous and unexpected laughter. All was clear. There was not even any "all" to obstruct the clarity. The statement of a contemporary spiritual teacher came to mind: "The real me is the whole universe." Instantly, the response arose: Why would one want any "me" at all, no matter how big it is? More laughter. And a sudden deep appreciation of the Prajnaparamita mantra: "Gone, gone, gone beyond, gone completely beyond." So this is what it points at.

During the evening service, this experience of transcendent Wisdom subtly began to enter the realm of the past, leaving me deeper, more joyous, more confident, but not yet actually Awake as Compassion and Wisdom. Shih-fu explained that he could not yet congratulate me, but predicted that sooner or later the unimaginable explosion would occur in which I utterly disappear. Leaving what?, one may ask. Leaving the Three Jewels, which are nothing but the all-consuming flames of Compassion and Wisdom. This is all that Master Sheng-Yen is in essence. May we disappear as he has, bearing Truth to all sentient beings.

Ch'an Retreat #2

On the first day of my second week-long meditation retreat with Master Sheng-Yen, the intensity of the kung-an, the repeated questioning "Who-am-I" continued at the high level that had developed during the first retreat, one month before. Shih-fu helped to sustain and deepen this intensity by asking me to practice as a matter of life and death, reminding me that one never knows when or if such an opportunity will present itself again in this lifetime.

Many times the question "Who-am-I" would burst into flames, and tears of spiritual commitment would spring from my eyes, almost turning to steam in the heat of my longing to get to the bottom of this primordial question which all beings are asking, consciously or unconsciously, and which even the universe itself is asking by its very existence. I did not feel caught up in an isolated personal quest but felt very near the center of the universal quest of human beings and, indeed, all conscious beings. But various spiritual experiences of peace and insight would arise and put out the flames of the kung-an, and I would suffer the illusion that these were answers to the question. Shih-fu relentlessly yet kindly attempted to turn my attention away from these spiritual experiences back to the sheer intensity of the practice "Who-am-I?"

These experiences were like wandering from the path to look at beautiful flowers or inspiring vistas. At this rate, one might never reach the end of the path. The master told me that

> "The thirty seconds of overwhelming intensity which threatened to shatter me that morning was miraculously sustained for about ten minutes. I felt like a warrior in life and death battle or like a wrathful Tantric Deity. 'I must discover who I am, I absolutely must, not for my own sake but to bring the Truth to all living beings.'"

if the flames of "Who-am-I?" die down, I must not simply accept this as part of the process but kindle them again with the torch of my own intense determination. The fire must become so vast that everything is consumed.

The talks Master Sheng-Yen gives during retreat are particularly potent for everyone, and convey important personal messages to each practitioner. This does not occur through the ordinary thinking process but, as Shih-fu himself says, is like throwing a ball that one must actually catch with the entire body and mind without knowing what direction this ball is coming from. On the second or third evening of the retreat, Master Sheng-Yen asked who had experienced sadness that day. I did not raise my hand because I had been experiencing simply the torrent of desperate longing for the Truth, interspersed with periods of peace and insight. But Shih-fu's message got through to the deeper layers of my being, because during the meditation period that followed the evening talk, I indeed experienced great sadness.

The problem I have of leaning slightly to the right during meditation began to concern me more deeply. This problem comes from years of sitting in meditation alone, with no one to correct my physical posture. But it is more than that. It dramatizes the deepest level of personal illusion, because when I am leaning to the right, I feel confident that I am perfectly upright. This illusion persists not only with eyes closed but also with my eyes completely open. Suddenly, I felt deep sadness that I do not know who I really am, that the ideas and perceptions about which I was so sure were not true. As I continued to ask the question "Who-am-I?" I shed tears of sadness from the heart rather than tears of determination from the will. I was asking the question more deeply than ever before. When I reported this experience to Master Sheng-Yen in his interview room, far from consoling me, he intensified my mood by stating clearly and convincingly that every thought and action since my very birth had been similarly off the mark — that I had lived my entire life in the realm of the false, imagining it to be true.

I accepted his statement and immediately felt a burden of intellectual and spiritual pride, that I was not even aware of carrying, fall away. With his subtle perception, Shih-fu saw that this purification had been accomplished, and he told me to forget the whole thing, that it was merely a mood, and I should simply return to the practice of "Who-am-I?"

Pushing forward more and more strongly with the kung-an, I often experienced the flames of determination raging for several hours on end. Finally, on the morning of the sixth day, with not only my whole mind but my whole body, with all its muscles and nerves, riveted on the question "Who-am-I?" there was a sudden release. The words clearly presented themselves: "There is nothing there." All tension dissolved as the phrase repeated itself: "There is nothing. There is nothing." There was a direct experience of what the Prajnaparamita Sutra teaches: there is really no body, no mind, no universe. I both laughed and wept as I experienced the radical nature of this resolution, or disappearance, of the question "Who-am-I?" A totally new realm presented itself, the realm of Prajnaparamita or Perfect Wisdom. For several hours I sat in utterly quiet and balanced meditation, but there was no I, no body sitting in the zendo, no process of meditation, no universe. As the heart sutra expresses it: "No wisdom, no attainment, no path." I felt no need to report this to Shih-fu, because it was perfectly clear and self-authenticating, and there really was no Shih-fu and nothing to report.

Master Sheng-Yen then asked all of us in turn, "Where is your mind?" I answered directly from the experience that nothing exists: "Nowhere!" Shih-fu asked me immediately: "Who says this?" Just as immediately, and with deep conviction, I answered: "Nobody!" Shih-fu again questioned: "What about the body that speaks these words?" The answer came: "There is no body!" The master turned aside and remarked: "Empty."

> "I saw the world in the opposite way from the habitual view of the conventional mind. I was sure that stones floated up into the sky and feathers plunged to the bottom of the ocean. The oxen were eating rice with chop-sticks and the farmers were grazing on grass. The children on the street were wielding the incense board and Shih-fu was throwing firecrackers in the zendo. I laughed and laughed and laughed…."

Just before this I had been doing fast walking (with no one walking and no zendo to walk in), when Shih-fu shouted "Stop!" Right before me was the scroll of Bodhidharma, and my eyes were gazing at the long fingernail on the third finger of his right hand. Shih-fu had then asked, "Where is your mind?" and I had answered inwardly, "In the third finger of Bodhidharma's right hand." When I told this to Master Sheng-Yen later, he said that this was a correct answer to the question, not the other series of answers I had given. He told me to let go of the experience of emptiness and continue to question "Who-am-I?" with strong effort.

Later that afternoon, on the final full day of retreat, I was to be led further into the realm of Ch'an towards which Bodhidharma's fingernail had been pointing. The realm of Ch'an is completely different from the perfect stillness and emptiness of Prajnaparamita, where one does not even experience peace, for there is no one to experience it. The realm of Ch'an is a realm of laughter. For several hours while seated in the meditation hall I was swept with wave after wave of laughter at the wonderful impossibility of everything. Given the Truth that nothing really exists, we are presented with an endlessly varied universe, whose existence is impossible yet whose appearance is vividly undeniable. The utterly quiet, primordial expanse of

Emptiness is continually surprised, as when a big stone is thrown into a still pond or colorful rockets explode in black space. Like a child, one can only laugh in sheer delight.

My brief foray into the realm of Ch'an was sparked by remembering a line from an ancient poem that Master Sheng-Yen had given me three years before. For one year I had only the Chinese. The following year Shih-fu gave me the translation, which was something like this:

The bridge is flowing and the stream is standing still. Beneath the water, the moon is shining, and fish are leaping in the sky.

It had been just a bizarre Zen poem to me then, but now, another year later, it became an igniting flame. I felt I might be going slightly crazy. I felt like a train that had left its tracks and was flying through the sky. I saw the world in the opposite way from the habitual view of the conventional mind. I was sure that stones floated up into the sky and feathers plunged to the bottom of the ocean. The oxen were eating rice with chop-sticks and the farmers were grazing on grass. The children on the street were wielding the incense board and Shih-fu was throwing fire-crackers in the zendo. I laughed and laughed and laughed, while the flow of "Who-am-I?" continued in the background. At one point, two cars on the street had a humorous conversation with their horns. I started laughing again, but this time the other meditators in the zendo began laughing with me. My laughter wasn't just subjective. The world really is this funny.

The Zen teaching-story came to mind about the master who killed a cat because none of his students could demonstrate the spirit of Ch'an in order to save it. Later, when his principal student returned from a journey, the Master asked him how he would have saved the cat. The student placed his own grass sandals on his head and walked out. The master remarked: "If he had been here, the cat would have been saved." I saw clearly the spirit of this action. Our habitual way of viewing the world must be reversed. Sandals belong on the head, not on the feet.

The last night of retreat, I sat in meditation right through till the dawn sitting, smoothly and deeply questioning "Who-am-I?" and refusing to allow myself to be diverted into spiritual experiences of any kind. No more tears, no more laughter. The next morning, I felt like a stick of incense burning in an empty room, like the sound of firecrackers in the streets, like a human being who eats and sleeps. What is there to realize?

The retreat was over, so there was no opportunity for an interview. But I'm sure Master Sheng-Yen would have said: "Return to the question, 'Who-am-I?'"

Lex Hixon (Nur al-Jerrahi) received his Ph.D. in World Religions from Columbia University in 1976. He then became an adept practitioner of several of the world's sacred traditions. From 1971 to 1984 he conducted a weekly radio show in New York City called "In The Spirit," interviewing spiritual teachers from around the world. An enlightened spiritual teacher, he guided many souls along their chosen path. Among his books are *Great Swan, Mother of the Universe, Heart of the Koran, Atom from the Sun of Knowledge, Mother of the Buddhas,* and *Living Buddha Zen*. For more information inquire at: www.lexhixon.org

Who Am I?

Who is asking the question?

There is nothing there.

There is nothing!

There is nothing!

No body, no mind,

No process of meditation

No wisdom, no attainment

No path – no universe!

Where is the mind?

Nowhere!

And the body that speaks the words?

Nobody!

Empty.

Gone, gone,

Gone beyond.

Gone completely beyond....

LLEWELLYN VAUGHN-LEE

MEDITATION ON THE LIFE-BREATH
The Simple Secret of Oneness

The following article is adapted from a talk by Llewellyn Vaughn-Lee, which addresses the deep need for seekers from all traditions to participate in the emerging work with oneness. How do we awaken within oneness? How do we work with the energy of oneness to help heal the wounds of the world so that our global community can begin manifesting the power, peace, and awareness that is our true nature? Vaughn-Lee explains that we begin with something simple, we begin with the breath combined with an innate sense of oneness.

"To those who are awake, the Cosmos is One."
Heraclitus

In our own inner practice we know that the energy of oneness is a powerful and transformative force, taking us beyond the conflicts and problems inherent in duality. How can we use our spiritual practice and awareness to help the whole world to awaken to its essential unity? When we awake within oneness we can participate in the spiritual work of the coming era — infusing the web of life, the magnificent Indra's net, with a spiritual consciousness that can nourish the whole and help our global community enter the next stage in its evolution.

The breath belongs to the esoteric core of much spiritual work and the processes of inner transformation. Just as breathing is fundamental to many forms of life, breath and the awareness of the breath is central to many spiritual practices, whether it is the simple meditation practice of watching your breath, repeating a *mantra*, or participating in *dhikr*.

Awareness of breath is awareness in the moment. When we are aware of the breath, we are not absorbed in the past, or in the future, but awake in the dynamic moment in which life is.

The importance of the awareness of breath is stressed in the Naqshbandi Sufi tradition by its founder, Baha-ad-din Naqshband: *"The foundation of our work is upon the breath. The more one is able to be conscious of one's breathing the stronger is one's inner life."*

Baha-ad-din gives particular significance to the space between the breaths, as does the Zen Buddhist practice of centering: *"The experience of one's reality may dawn between two breaths. As breath turns from down to up, and again as breath curves from up to down — through both these turns, realize."*

Awareness of the breath is one of the most powerful agents of spiritual transformation and yet we are only aware of part of its potency. What is it we realize in the turns of the breath, and how does the cycle of the breath help bring the light and consciousness of oneness into the world?

The In-breath

Spiritual masters have long understood how the cycle of the breath enacts the journey to the source and back into the world. The in-breath takes us inward, back to the source. This is why in most instances the last breath of a dying person is an in-breath, that final gasp of air as the soul goes back to its source and does not return into this world.

With every breath we take we make this return journey, before the out-breath brings us back into life. If one is very attentive one can experience an instant of bliss at the end of the in-breath which is akin to the bliss of the Self, what Vedanta calls Atman. This instant of bliss is felt in the *Anandamaya kosha*, the sheath of the apparently individualized soul, and gives us a glimpse of what it is like to be free from time, awake in the timeless realm of the Soul, in the love and peace that is our real nature — what is waiting for us at the end of the journey.

The spiritual path draws us inward towards our real nature. This is the journey that most people associate with spiritual life, the journey back to the source in which we free ourselves from the grip of the ego and its illusions and discover our true self. On the Sufi path one is drawn inward through the pain of longing, the lover longing for her Beloved. We are drawn away from the ego and outer world of appearances, the illusions of the world, to find the truth that is within our own hearts.

Much of the work of the path is a process of uncovering, peeling away the skins of the onion. We discover the multiple layers of our personality, ego and psyche that separate us from our true nature. This is not a linear progression, but a dance of unveiling — an often bewildering, confusing dance that is really a relationship of ourself to our Self, which happens through the practices and energy of the path.

Gradually the veils of separation begin to lift and we discover the luminous center of our own nature, *"the face before I was born."* This is the Self, what is real beneath all the illusions, what is waiting for us at the end of the journey. This spiritual quest is described in Attar's *The Conference of the Birds*, the classic Sufi story of thirty birds searching for the mystical Simorgh, (si-morgh also means thirty birds). At the end of the journey they experience who they really are:

Their souls rose free of all they'd been before.
The past and all its actions were no more.
Their life came from that close, insistent sun
And in its vivid rays they shone as one.
In the Simorgh's radiant face they saw Themselves.
The Simorgh of the world — with awe
They gazed, and dared at last to comprehend
They were the Simorgh and the journey's end.

The thirty birds discover that they are the Simorgh, the object of their quest. The greatest journey takes us back to the simple and yet astounding truth of who we really are. And on this journey the Self is continually revealing itself in different ways. One such glimpse may be an unexpected moment of deep peace, for the Self is a state of peace. This is a peace that does not result from any outer situation or belong to any conflict resolution because it does not belong to pairs of opposites. It is a peace that is ever-present. As Ramana Maharshi has said, *"We are always peace. To get rid of the idea that we are not peace is all that is required."*

At the beginning this may just be a moment of this peace, then it may last for days. Finally it is present under all of our activities. We just have to look under the surface and we can rest in the peace of our Self. It is a quality of being that is always with us. It is also traditionally the gift of a great teacher to his disciples, as Christ gave to His disciples: *"Peace I leave with you, my peace I give to you, not as the world giveth, give I unto you."*

The Self has other qualities. For example real freedom and unconditional love. On the level of the Self there is no judgment, but compassion, complete acceptance and pure love. Our real being is also a dynamic state of oneness, of unity. When we discover ourselves we discover that we are one with the Self and one with everything. We are a state of unity. In us everything is united, everything is whole. This is the circle of wholeness that belongs to all of life. Nothing is excluded.

The Self is the multifaceted diamond, the mandala that includes all aspects of life, the beggar and the king, the laughter and the teardrop. It is all one. And our individual self is the universal Self. We are one with the stars and the cosmos as well as with every snowflake, and the cry of every child.

The awakening of the Self is an awakening to an all-embracing oneness that is at first intoxicating, awe-inspiring and yet completely natural. Resting in the Self we rest in this oneness. It is a state of being. Often an initial experience of the Self is a state of being or presence, full of the simple wonder of being human. We feel we are present in a reality beyond duality, beyond this world of opposites. And when we fully awake in the Self we experience pure Consciousness that is nondual. It is. It knows. There is no subject or object — only oneness. The pure Consciousness of the awakened Self is the light of Oneness.

And then the mystical path takes us even further: beyond the Self into the emptiness; beyond its dazzling light into the dazzling darkness; beyond the state of being into the states of nonbeing; the uncreated emptiness. While the Self is a reality of light and pure consciousness, nonbeing belongs to darkness and unknowing. This is what Thomas Merton describes as *"desert and void."*

The Uncreated is waste and emptiness to the creature: not even sand; not even stone; not even darkness and night. A burning wilderness would at least be "something." It burns and is wild. But the Uncreated is no something. Waste. Emptiness. Total poverty of the Creator; yet from this poverty springs everything. The waste is inexhaustible. Infinite Zero. Everything comes from this desert. Nothing. Everything wants to return to it and cannot. For who can return nowhere?

For those who want to be lost, this nothingness is waiting. And then further than the uncreated emptiness, than the states of nonbeing, is Ultimate Reality about which nothing can be said except that it is other than anything, and destroys every concept, every idea, every notion of what is and what is not.

The Out-breath

The inner journey takes the wayfarer into the dimension of the Self and beyond. But this is only half of the story. It is only the in-breath. With every in-breath there is an out-breath, a turn from the inner worlds to the outer worlds. In our focus on the inner journey we often overlook or forget the potency of the out-breath, and yet it is central to the miracle of creation.

On the out-breath light, love, and spiritual nourishment flow from the source into life. Life is sustained by the continual flow of energy from the inner. And we are a part of this flow. We are not separate from life. Through our breath the real world of the inner sustains the outer world of forms. Just as we are continually sustained by the energy of the Self, so is the world sustained by the energy of the Real that comes from the inner. If there were no flow of energy the world would dissolve, become just a fading mirage. The Sufis call this sustaining energy of the Real the secret of the word *Kun!* (Be!). It is the hidden secret of the world.

As the veils of separation fall away we experience what is real within life, we begin to see His face in His creation. Our outer life becomes richer, more meaningful. Rather than being caught in the past or the future, in dreams and desires, we are present in life as it is. In Zen this is often experienced in a moment of *satori,* when we are present in the beauty and wonder of the moment, see the blossom on the tree, feel the rain falling, without thought or judgment. For an instant we are really alive.

Through the mystery of the out-breath, the energy of the Self sustains and transforms us and our life. And the more our awareness is grounded in the Self rather than the ego, the more we experience this nourishment. In fact, our awareness enables the Self to participate more directly in our life. Through our conscious alignment with the Real It comes into our life or reveals Itself in our life. This is the significance of our practices and participation in the process, what the Sufi calls *"polishing the mirror of the heart."* This polishing enables the light of the real sun to be reflected into our life. This light nourishes both our own life and life around us. This has traditionally been part of the work of the wayfarer — to bring the light of what is real into life.

The individual brings light into his immediate surroundings as he journeys Home, cleaning his own backyard and making a real contribution to his inner and outer environment. However, there is a larger dimension of spiritual work that traditionally belongs to the *Bodhisattva* model, the one who renounces the fruits of enlightenment for the sake of humanity and the world.

This bigger dimension of nourishing the whole of life is associated with the individual who has traversed the entire inner journey and then returns to the world. We first return to the source, and then work for the well-being of the whole. This is beautifully imaged in the Zen Ox-Herding pictures. After capturing and taming the bull of one's lower nature, one *"returns to the root and the source."* Then, in the final image, the old man comes back to the market-place:

> *Barefoot and naked of breast,*
> *I mingle with the people of the world.*
> *My clothes are ragged and dust laden,*
> *and I am ever blissful.*
> *I use no magic to extend my life;*
> *Now before me, the dead trees become alive.*
>
> *I go to the market place with my wine bottle*
> *and return home with my staff.*
> *I visit the wine shop and market,*
> *and everyone I look upon becomes enlightened.*

This is the classical image of those who, having discovered their true nature, live from this source and naturally transform life. They are no longer interested in their own spiritual transformation, but around them *"the dead trees become alive."* Traditionally it takes at least twenty to thirty years of dedicated practice under the guidance of a teacher to make this journey. In the Ox-Herding pictures the young man who went in search of the bull has become an old man when he returns to the market-place.

The Need of the Time

However, at this moment in time, as the world appears to be dying through our exploitation and greed, there is a deep need for the energy of the Real to be given to the whole of life, to nourish and transform it. There is spiritual work to be done by those who have not yet completed the journey, who have been given a glimpse of their real nature, of their divine self, but still remain in the ego rather than resting in what is real.

At this moment of time we can each directly participate in the spiritual work for the whole, in the out-breath of life. All that is needed is that we recognize this larger dimension of spiritual work and no longer focus only on our individual inner journey or spiritual well-being. We must consciously live the whole cycle of the breath.

This shift is not so easy for seekers who have identified spiritual work solely with the journey Home, the journey back to the Source. But our world is crying out for the energy of what is real. And it needs our help.

We have collectively forgotten that the world is sacred, that it is an expression of the out-breath of the divine. The world has become so covered in illusions that it is starving, dying, and its sacred meaning is falling away. It is covered in a cloud of forgetfulness so dense that it is difficult for the energy of the Real to shine through. It is dying.

And sadly, although many people are aware of the ecological state of the world they do not glimpse the inner truth of how we have denied our spiritual heritage and created an inner wasteland, which is reflected in outer pollution and a sense of meaninglessness. Instead of an inner attitude of respecting the sacred essence of life, we have created a wasteland of desire and greed, an underlying attitude that the world is here to fulfill us.

We have also created a collective illusion of separation: we are separate from each other and conditioned to focus on our own individual prosperity. We are separate from the world and it does not matter how we treat it, how we pollute it to fulfill our desires. And even many people who engage in spiritual practice remain caught in the collective attitude of greed and desire, wanting something for themselves rather than engaging in a real egoless quest or life of service. Through our self-indulgence we have neglected our responsibility to honor the sacredness in life and its intrinsic wholeness.

So much has been desecrated and lost that there is desperate need for those who have glimpsed the light of the Real to help bring its light into the world. The world needs to be awakened from a dream that is killing it.

How can we work to bring the light of the Self into the world? How can we fully participate in the spiritual out-breath of life? Once we step outside of the illusion of our own separate self, a radically different picture emerges. We have been conditioned by our culture to believe that we are each a separate individual, and as a result we often feel alone and isolated, impotent to effect real change. However, a glimpse of the Self gives us a sense of an interconnected oneness in which nothing is separate: everything is an expression of a oneness that is dynamically alive. Every person, every stone, is this oneness. In this oneness everything is connected and interdependent. Our individual Self is the Universal Self and it is all a living organism of light and love.

When we live with conscious awareness of our intrinsic oneness we bring this oneness into a collective consciousness that is dying through the illusion of separation. Our light is the light of the world; our divine consciousness is the spiritual consciousness of the world — nothing is separate.

Only the divine can change and heal the world; only the energy and power of the Real can free the world from its self-destructive illusions. And this energy and awareness of the Real is within each of us, is each of us. When we turn away from the ego and its desires, we know that we are the Real. And we are also life hungry for what is real. In the dynamic interconnected whole, we are the in-breath and out-breath of life — a life that is not just physical existence, but a multidimensional living organism of light and love. We are the spiritual life-blood of the planet and we need to honor this dimension of life, this quality of oneness that is present within everything.

Awakening to Oneness

Part of the esoteric mystery of life is that the individual is a microcosm of the whole. This means that just as the individual can awaken to an awareness of the oneness of the Self, the whole world can also awaken to oneness. This is the possibility of this present time, as one era comes to an end and another begins. Just as the world is at a stage of crisis, so are there the indications of an awakening in the dawning of a global consciousness and tools like the internet which mirror the dynamic interconnected wholeness of life. The whole world has the potential to awaken.

As each individual brings the awareness of the Self into life, we can see that the light of our individual Self is not separate but forms part of the spiritual body of the planet, because just as the individual has a spiritual body made of light, so does the planet. The light of the Self is the greatest contribution we can make to life, because this light does not belong to duality and its conflict-creating dynamics.

The pure light of the Self belongs to the dimension of oneness, and it can bring the awareness of oneness into our collective consciousness and all of life. This light can banish the illusion of separation and help humanity to see the web of life of which we are a part. Once we see this web and are awake to its potential, then we will respond in a very different way to the apparent problems of the present time. Once we collectively realize that we are one living organism, then many of our attitudes will change. Seen with the eyes of oneness, many of our present problems will disappear. For example, there is enough food to feed the planet in an ecologically sustainable manner: it is only worldly power dynamics that prevent this from happening.

Oneness is not an ideal but a living dynamic reality that belongs to our true nature and to all of life. And the awareness of oneness that belongs to the Self is an inherent part of life. When we bring this awareness into life we help life to awaken to its true nature, as a self-sustaining organism that has its own spiritual consciousness.

How do we live the awareness of oneness? The first step is to acknowledge the light of oneness within us. Through the in-breath we glimpse the light of the Self or feel its qualities of peace, bliss, or its infinite nature. Then through the out-breath we bring it into life. Through this we recognize our own divine nature and the sacred dimension of life and know that they are one. We say "yes" to what is real within us and recognize the need that life has for this energy of the real.

That which is real is much more powerful than life's illusions. All we need is a taste; all we need is a simple moment of connection, a moment of being with the breath, who we are. It is difficult for many of us to realize that individually we have the power to change our collective forgetfulness, to help the world to awaken. Part of the power dynamics of our culture is to disenfranchise the individual, and create the illusion that real power is only in the hands of large corporations or political organizations. But when we experience the reality of the Self we know the illusory nature of worldly power, how it is as fragile as the ego. We experience a power that is real:

"*That boundless Power, source of every power, manifesting itself as life, entering every heart, living there among the elements yet free of them — that is Self.*"

We have denied ourselves our mystical heritage, and forgotten the potency of spiritual power. We need to reclaim this direct power that is within each of us. Then, by the simple practice of awareness and an inner attitude of service it can be given back to life.

Human beings are powerful transformers of energy. Through our spiritual centers we are connected to the spiritual energies of the inner worlds that sustain us. Through us, love and power come from the inner into the outer world of which we are a part. And a network of individuals linked together in love and service to the whole is many times more powerful than a single person. If we work together for the sake of the whole, we create an organic, nonhierarchical network of light that can bypass many of the centralized systems which appear to control our world. Energy can flow freely and unrestricted into life where it is needed, healing the planet, awakening the world to its own true nature.

We have been conditioned to separate the spiritual from life: this is part of the dualistic conditioning of the past era that has, so to speak, "*banished the divine into heaven and left us alone in the world.*" Our focus on the journey home is part of this dynamic. But we no longer have to believe that we are separate. If we are not separate, where is there to go?

We have forgotten that our spiritual light is a part of life and connects us to the whole. We need to reclaim our deep knowing of how the visible and invisible worlds work together; how love flows from emptiness into form; how in each breath the sacred dimension of life is born anew; and how we are part of the light of oneness that is being born anew in each moment, in the potential of each moment. This is not something we need to achieve or struggle for, but is present in each breath, in who we are.

Let us say "yes" to the need of the moment, to life's hunger for the light of oneness. Through the simple practice of being attentive and present in life, through being aware of the in-breath and the out-breath, we can respond to this need. We can bring the light of oneness that is within each of us into life. We can help the world awaken to its true nature.

Llewellyn Vaughn-Lee is a Sufi teacher and author. In recent years the focus of his writing and teaching has been on spiritual responsibility in our present time of transition, and the emerging global consciousness of oneness. He has also specialized in the area of dreamwork, integrating the ancient Sufi approach to dreams with the insights of modern psychology. He is the founder of The Golden Sufi Center *(www.goldensufi.org)*. Among his published books are **Working with Oneness** and **Light of Oneness**.

◆ SWAMI ASESHANANDA

MEDITATION & THE GOAL OF LIFE
The Natural Destination of Rapt Contemplation

The following discourse was delivered by the late Swami Aseshanandaji Maharaj on the podium of the Vedanta Society of Portland, Oregon, in 1986.

The subject of my talk this morning is Meditation and The Goal of Life. When I think of the goal of life I think of Saint Paul. Paul is the second founder of Christianity. And it is Paul who has given Christians the idea of original sin, as well as salvation as the goal of life. But when I think of salvation I think of resurrection, and resurrection always conveys the idea of a post-mortem emancipation. And then you get a new body, and a new heaven, and so forth.

But that does not satisfy me. Going to heaven while thinking of the future will not be in tune with Shankaracharya's philosophy. He does not accept the idea of freedom in a future lifetime to be the supreme goal of life. *Jivanmukti!* You must be free here and now. You are to attain freedom in this life, in this body, and you can do that because you are potentially divine. But you will have to get rid of the idea of sinfulness, of your ego, of your loneliness, and get rid of the problem of spiritual passivity. And that is what Swami Vivekananda came to the West to preach. *"Ye divinities on earth, it is the greatest sin to call another a sinner."*

And here, a method becomes necessary; every goal needs a way. You cannot reach any goal unless you follow a proven path. And the path to us is the *Jnanamarga*, the way of wisdom to the supreme Self. This will succeed. But it is the *Bhaktimarga*, devotion alone, that has been accepted by Western man. If you read the Bible's interpretation, without Christ there can be no salvation. Similarly, the Old Testament tells you that without Moses and the Prophets there can be no good, working religion.

But all this is based in mythology. What you experience in your own life is pleasure and pain; what you experience in your own life is youthful optimism and old age pessimism; what you encounter in your own life is success and failure. Today you have a job, tomorrow, no job. Today you have a home, tomorrow, no home. This is called the "dual throng"; you are tossed about in the dual throng because you live with the belief that time is real.

When I consider time in the Western way of thinking, then I have to think of Saint Augustine. It is Augustine who has given Western man what is called "the linear view of time." In this way the West has accepted what I call the reality of the world; time is real, the world is real, and particularly, the pragmatic view of the West, is that your society is real.

The goal of Western man is what you mean when you talk of progress. Progress here means your dissatisfaction with the old and acceptance with what is new – which you think to be better. This idea of progress the West has taken from the Greeks. And this idea of progress is connected with intellectualism. Especially, this is the gift of science and technology. Protestant countries have accepted science as the key to the solution of all the problems of life, as well as of death.

And so, the West has embraced progress. That is why a 1986 car will be old-fashioned when the 1987 model is released. Do something new! Whether that new thing will be dutiful or unstable, it makes no difference. Something new: that is what people want here. After a few months they will go to a beauty salon and change the color of their hair; the old color will have to go. (laughter) You see, I have no objection to progress, but I insist that progress must be measured in terms of moral development and spiritual edification. Progress, otherwise, makes you think in terms of time. Then time is real.

But if you belong to the world of time you cannot attain your timeless perfection. The goal of a good Christian who follows the words of Jesus in the Sermon on the Mount should be perfection, not progress. What do I mean by perfection? Change....less....ness. Anything that changes is not perfect. *"Be thee therefore perfect as thy Father in Heaven"* means spiritual perfection. The world can never be perfect. Since the West has accepted the Greek philosophy of life, it has therefore accepted the myth of social perfection. This is leading to the Star Wars phenomena. (laughter) Billions of dollars spent on that, while poverty and human suffering lie untended outside the studio doors. There are unhappy homes. These psychopathic hospitals are full. And divorce rates have gone skyhigh. Is this your progress? Where there is no certainty, where there is no stability, where there is no inner strength and conviction to think of the supreme Goal of life – what I call spiritual emancipation – *Jivanmukti* – there can be no satisfaction. Therefore, the *Bhogamarga* of Western man will spell disaster, as it always has in the past.

We Vedantists speak about Truth, about real Life, and about strength based upon individual independence. If people come to listen, well and good. If people do not come, we will talk to the walls. [laughter] ....the walls will have ears.

So, here, this is the message. Build your life. I understand that India has developed tremendously. I have not seen India since 1947. India is not the same India of my youth. Nowadays it has got television [laughter]. It did not have television back then. But I ask India not to forget its spiritual strength, which comes not from television, but from God-vision, and from keeping the flag of renunciation hoisted. For, if India cannot produce illumined souls, then India will be just like Japan or any other nation. That means it will imitate the West and will produce what is called scientific technology, but will not be able to produce illumined souls.

In my early days I saw an illumined soul; I saw Ramana Maharshi with my own eyes. Although he did not belong to our Order, he had great love for our Order. He was really a good man, a noble man. I took him some mangoes, and he had them washed, and sliced them with his own hands. Then he distributed them and took some himself. I was very pleased. He was an Advaitin. Therefore, who is an Advaitin? One who practices renunciation and realizes the truth that his real nature is infinite, not finite. The dualistic religion of the West needs Advaita, called nonduality. But the Church will not accept it. The Church is conservative; it will remain loyal only to the theology of Paul.

And that is the reason why there is a kind of eagerness in the minds of the people today to live the life, realize the truth, and to be established in the domain of spirituality which the world of maya will not be able to enter.

Now I will speak of *guru-shakti*. Then comes the *mantra-shakti*. The relationship of the *guru* and disciple is established through the *mantra*, the sacred word. When the *guru* gives the *mantra* he is in a higher state of consciousness; but the disciple is not in that state. Gross, subtle, causal, and the transcendental state of *Turiya*. If you read Shankaracharya's scriptures you will understand. Gross level means when you are body conscious; food conscious. Higher than that is when we think thoughts of love, goodwill, thoughts of sympathy. This is the thought level. Then higher than the thought level is the causal level. That is when you long for the vision of God.

Sri Ramakrishna used to cry out at the end of each day, "*Another day has passed and I have not seen Thee, Oh Mother. How long will I have to wait?*" A drowning man longs for a breath of air. Just like that, the devotee must long for God. A devotee is not satisfied with merely hearing lectures about God. He wants God in his own life. Therefore he meditates. He performs all his works and offers them to the Lord.

So here, there is intense activity blended in with intense calmness of mind. It is not that only through meditation that you will be able to reach perfection, or the Goal of life. All the four yogas need to be combined. That means, you must be intellectually bright, your heart must be cheerful and energetic, and you must also long for the vision of God. This longing will come when the mind becomes pure. "Pure" means conscious of the need for realization. That is akin to what you find in St. John of the Cross's "dark night of the soul." The dark night means the need for detachment from the world of comfort. Sadhana must be taken up and connected to Grace. Then, depending upon His Will, the heart's desire may be fulfilled.

Someone here once asked me this question: Why all this thinking about the personal God? It is necessary because man at present is a person, so he can understand only when the personal aspect of God is revealed to him. And that is why the personal aspect of God is called *ekagrata*; *ekagrata* means one-pointed mind. And the impersonal God according to Patanjali, is the *nirudha* state, when you have transcended mind. This state according to Gaudapada is called *amanibhava*, or mindlessness. This should not be interpreted as being there is "no mind," thus no thought. No. When thinker, thought, and the object of thought are one, that is the idea. *Triputibedha*.

Whatever the case, the truth is that without the power of renunciation one will not be able to think of God. Everything else will come, but not That. [laughter] The singular thought of God comes when mind is pure. Therefore, meditation is really *tailadharadhyan*, like an unbroken line of oil poured from one vessel to another. So meditation does not mean when you go into the shrine or the church and sit. No. Meditation will be a continual process. So when you are walking, eating, doing some garden work, or when you are meditating, your higher mind is at the forefront and your sense-bound mind has been rejected. It means you have withdrawn yourself from your sense-bound mind and have accepted sense-free mind, called *sattvic* mind.

And that is what the great teachers have said, "*ahar shuddho shanta shanti.*" That is Sanatkumara's saying. When your thoughts are pure, your mind-stuff will be pure. When the mind-stuff is pure there will be constant remembrance of the presence of God. And when there is this constancy there will be realization of God, you see. And that is what Holy Mother used to say: "*Do japa; meditate upon the spiritual form of the Ishtam, the Chosen Ideal, in the shrine of your own heart.*" For what purpose? Again, *Kundalini jagarana*: to awaken the shakti power within that is lying there asleep.

> "....you should know for certain that spiritual power will not awaken due to asana and pranayam. Spiritual awakening will come from sense-control, not from breath control. Self control is necessary, not lung control. The body-bound westerner will not learn this."

You know, a little breathing exercise may be needed at the outset, but you should know for certain that spiritual power will not awaken due to *asana* and *pranayama*. Spiritual awakening will come from sense control, not from breath control. Self-control is necessary, not mere lung control. The body-bound Westerner will not learn this.

But working to gain a pure mind transcends all this. Otherwise there will come *vikshipta*, restless mind. Breath control or not, sense control or not, your mind still remains restless, yes? You have a scattered mind, which shows that your thinking process is rajasic. If the mind is sattvic then concentration will come quite easily. And the happiness you have after comes from concentration. This is another thing the Westerner will not understand, you see? Careful! It all may be going to the dogs!

Once we were driving and I saw a van that had a sign on it that read, "Going to the dogs." I thought, what does that mean, for I knew it was an expression of failure and so forth. So I asked a devotee, what does that mean? He told me that it was a dog food company's van. I thought that there must be some very happy dogs out there to have their food delivered to them so willingly. [laughter]

But man cannot be happy with food alone. He must eat to live, not live to eat. He has an ideal; an ideal of freedom that never occurs in animals. It should become the foremost idea of every human being to become free. This freedom, called *moksha*, will confer real satisfaction to myself, to my friends, to my parents, to my relatives, and to all those who know me. Do you believe me? If not, look around and see if you have ever brought total satisfaction to anyone in your lifetime. India has *gulam pavitram:* if a man attains illumination, realizes God, his family for generations will become purified. They will escape the horrible bondages of this old world. His mother will be gratified.

Swamiji's mother came to the Belur Math in the early days. She was so proud, saying, "See what my Naren has done!" But he said, "No mother; the Great Master has done all this. It was the old man's doing." [laughter] This is the sign of *guru-bhakti.* This is missing in the west, though not completely. But the Church has not accepted it; the need of a guru it has not accepted. Only the Savior can give salvation, they say, while you or other illumined souls cannot give it to yourself. But India has seen hundreds and thousands of self-realized souls.

So the Church, with its Savior complex, has taken the place of the guru. But, interestingly enough, it is the guru who guides over those centuries when the Savior does not appear. The individual is not encouraged to seek direct realization of God; it is enough to accent the doctrines of the Church. It would be disloyal to the Church to find your own way. In India, you see, the Church is a means to an end. That is why Swamiji said, *"It is good to be born in a church, but do not die in one."* You see, the entire matter is, ultimately, the *"flight of the alone to the alone"* as the *Upanisads* state.

So, personal self-effort is important. There is no infallible church or infallible organization. They all have certain flaws, or defects. And so you have souls who desire freedom, not dependance. If monastic life is to be uplifted, if the monastery is to be edified, then monks, themselves, should think in terms of realization of God and service of God in mankind. That is *atmano mokshartha jagad hitaya cha – for the realization of the Atman and the highest good of the world.* This cannot be done merely by joining an organization. It is a personal decision that has individual motivation behind it, personal inspiration, and personal determination.

And so you will find, then, that the Goal of Life is the realization of God. Acceptance of dogmas and creeds will not be sufficient. Here, the church should not be the mediator; but guru can be the mediator. So let guru be the mediator, and let the individual be the meditator. [laughter]

Take for example, I have got three gurus. And I pay my respects to all of them. Holy Mother gave my initiation; Swami Brahmananda gave my *brahmacharya,* and Swami Saradananda gave me my *sannyas.* But my primary guru is called the *diksha guru.* She was the one who gave me my mantra and started me on the path towards illumination. It changed my life, changed my outlook also. It drove me towards freedom, the Goal of Life.

America has a noble heritage. It sought to free itself from the tyranny of Europe. But this freedom should encourage them to seek spiritual freedom. And that freedom cannot come after death; it must come here and now. We must not think about the future. Trust no future, no matter how pleasant.

You cannot realize God unless your are Godlike. The inner life must be charged with the fire of spirituality, and this awakening must then inspire every step. And we must not be satisfied until we have reached the goal. That is why, *prashanta manasa yenum, prashantam manasam* – the mind must become calm, utterly calm; that is the first requisite. If you see the fault of others then the mind will never be calm. This is because God dwells in the inmost heart of every person. Our attitude towards all must be holy.

So the power of the mantra will change all the samskaras; all the mental impressions will become purified. After that, then, open the door. God consciousness cannot come if we are only conscious of human beings. The difference between subject and object prevails there, you see. So turning inward, the devotee beholds his pure ego and attains *Savikalpa samadhi.* That unveils the personal aspect of God. But when you transcend the pure ego and behold the Atman, that is *Nirvikalpa Samadhi.* This is the Oneness of Existence that will reveal the divinity of mankind. That is the Mt. Everest of realization. In this you realize the true nature of Self.

And so you see, when this realization comes, the river has entered into the sea. All longing has been fulfilled. Man has then reached perfection. This is also called *Brahmanirvana* in the Gita. Others speak about emptiness, *Shunyata.* I do not accept emptiness. What? Your final attainment will be entering into a void? That does not appeal to me. It is fulfilment; it is plenum; it is *purnata,* not *shunyata.*

And so, the realization of perfection in this very life is the goal of a Christian, the goal of a Hindu, the goal of a scientist, the goal of a philosopher, and for that we must bend all our efforts and keep awake the spirit of love, the spirit of faith, and the spirit of understanding that man is the greatest symbol, the greatest expression of the divine Spirit.

This realization will prompt the individual, and help him to bend all his efforts for *sarvamukti.* First one has to attain *Jivanmukti,* his own personal liberation. But you also have to do some great good to your fellow human beings. So spend all your days and nights with unbroken zeal and honesty, and pray to God sincerely, and say, "May all be illumined, may all see the face of Truth, may all go beyond the darkness of maya and taste the delight of immortality and freedom in this very life.

Thank you.

Swami Aseshananda, a direct disciple of Sri Sarada Devi, Sri Ramakrishna's wife and spiritual consort, was the Spiritual Minister of the Vedanta Society of Portland for over forty years. He also received holy company with some of the direct disciples of the Great Master. He is the author of *Glimpses of a Great Soul,* on the life and teachings of Swami Saradananda.

SRI SARADA TRANSMISSION
Reminiscences by Two of Her Direct Monastic Disciples

Swami Nityasvarupananda

It was on the day of December 23, 1916, that Swami Mahadevananda and I went to Holy Mother's house at Bagbhazar. At once we went to the Ganges, had our bath, returned to the Holy Mother's house, and were waiting to bow to Her. At that time the Holy Mother was worshiping Sri Ramakrishna in the shrine on the first floor. We were waiting on the ground floor. Swami Mahadevananda, who was quite at home there, went upstairs to see what the Holy Mother was doing. By then the Holy Mother had finished Her worship, but was still seated in the shrine where She was worshiping Sri Ramakrishna. Swami Mahadevananda made his obeisance to Her and then came back downstairs and told me that the Holy Mother was still seated in the shrine after Her worship. He asked me to go upstairs and make my obeisance to Her. I went upstairs and entered the shrine and made my obeisance to Her. The moment I bowed to Her, She looked at me and said, "Well, will you have initiation?" I was overwhelmed. She immediately said to me, "Take your seat. Perform *achamana*." Then She said, "Which God or Goddess do you love the most?" I immediately told the Holy Mother the name of my only God. She then gave me initiation.

I had not taken any gift with me to offer at Her feet, as is the custom at the time of initiation, for I did not know that my initiation would take place in this manner. The Holy Mother asked me to bring some fruits from those under Her bed in the shrine room. Accordingly, I brought some and She asked me to offer them at Her feet, which I did. Then I bowed to Her, left the room, went downstairs, and told Swami Mahadevananda all that had happened.

After my initiation, a friend of mine and I went out and bought a piece of cloth with a very narrow red border, the kind of cloth the Holy Mother used to wear. We also purchased some grapes. They were then offered to the Holy Mother. At noontime I had *prasad* at the Holy Mother's house.

Swami Mahadevananda told me that after I had had my initiation, the Holy Mother said to him, "This boy will make his mother and brothers weep," indicating thereby that I was meant for the life of renunciation.

Swami Aseshananda

That compass, that eternal guide of my soul, is the Holy Mother. I met Her for the first time at the office of Udbodhan, Calcutta, in 1917. It was *darshan* day. Hundreds of people assembled downstairs in the Holy Mother's house for *darshan* of the Mother. Swami Dhirananda suggested to me, "When you go see the Holy Mother, request Her to bless you out of Her unbounded grace." But when I was ushered into the Mother's presence, I was forbidden to speak at all by the brahmachari who was one of the guides. After having Mother's *darshan*, I reported to Swami Dhirananda that I was not allowed to speak to the Mother. At this the swami called Swami Arupananda, who again took me upstairs to the very presence of the Mother. This time the Mother had no veil on Her face. She heard from Swami Arupananda that I visited Swami Brahmananda quite often. She said to Arupananda, "Rakhal is quite competent to give him initiation. Let him ask Rakhal." To this I said very humbly, "Mother, it will be a great good fortune for me if you kindly initiate me and bless me." Mother agreed. She fixed a time, asked me to fast, take my bath in the Ganges and wait patiently downstairs.

Mother, after finishing Her worship of the divine Master, called me through a monk. I was asked to sit on a seat next to Her in the shrine. She asked a few questions about my spiritual life to which I replied correctly. After deep meditation, Mother imparted to me the sacred mystic Name (*bija-mantra*). I felt the power of the mantra as a vehicle of *guru-shakti* at that moment. The previous night I had wondered whether Mother would be able to choose the *Ishta* (Chosen Deity) for whom I had shown reverence from my boyhood. To my great surprise She chose the *Istha* whom I liked very much. I did not say anything. Mother knew my heart, for She is *antaryamini*. Through Her grace I have come to realize that one can get direct experience of God in this life if one is earnest, sincere, and whole-hearted.

Today, nearly seventy years later, I feel vividly that Mother is alive in my consciousness, that Her divine hand is on my head to carry me across the ocean of *Samsara* to the realm of eternal Light and Felicity.

◆ LEX HIXON

TALK WITH MAEZUMI ROSHI
The Import of Training & Zen Transmission

On November 26th, 1978, Lex Hixon hosted Maezumi Roshi of the LA Zen Center at WBAI Radio in New York City. The opening announcements of the program are included to give some context and atmosphere regarding New York City in the 1970's.

Maezumi Roshi from the LA Zen Center is here with us in the studio this morning and we are going to really have a deep conversation about Zen and to do a kind of meditation. The Roshi will give a kind of Zen talk, which will afford us a chance for real meditation, and then he will take some dharma interviews over the air. So, if you do have any friends who are interested in Zen, or interested in one of the most important spiritual leaders of this country, give them a call and tell them to tune in – 99.5 FM.

Just to make a couple of announcements to begin with: some interesting things happening in the City this week. One of the most important, of course, is Maezumi Roshi here and tomorrow evening, Monday, November 27th at 6:00pm, the Roshi will be giving a talk at Japan House. That is at 333 East 47th Street. Some of you heard the program last week with Bernie Glassman Sensei, who is a dharma successor of the Roshi. He is actually a Zen teacher himself. It was a good program. I do not usually refer back to a previous week's program but I think that anyone who is interested in Zen in the West, and just in general in the spiritual development of the culture, might be interested to hear a tape of that program. The cassette tapes are available through *In the Spirit*. Telephone number is 966-0554. Among other things, Bernie Glassman Sensei gave a dharma talk on "The Sound of One Hand," and the Sh'ma, "Hear O Israel, God is One," a very beautiful combination. So he will be giving a talk this Friday, December 1st, at 8:00pm, at the Dharma Dhatu, a Dharma center which is at 49 East 21st Street. So those of you who are particularly attracted to having an American teach in Zen, to see what that would be like, go hear his talk. Finally, Maezumi Roshi will give another talk on Saturday, December 2nd, at 8:00pm at the Universalist Church, which is at 4 West 76th Street. So, these are three dharma talks by these two friends who come from Los Angeles to meet with some of the parents of their students at the LA Zen Center. It has been a great delight to know them. They both are very, very authentic teachers. That gives you a real choice – these three talks – one by Maezumi Roshi and one by Bernie Glassman Sensei. If the announcements go by you too fast, you can always call 966-0554, the *In the Spirit* number. You can call any time this afternoon or during the week and these announcements can be clarified for you.

One or two other things that are happening this week – Tuesday, a very, very delightful and almost unimaginable person from Denmark named Ole is going to be giving a Dharma talk at a Dharma center on the upper West Side at 498 West End Avenue at 84th Street – Tuesday at 8:00pm. I think he is one of the most eloquent and beautiful and believably enthusiastic westerners who can speak about Buddha Dharma and do it in a way that has an immediate impact. He is going to be showing some color slides. He is like a western embodiment of Tibetan Buddhist tradition. It should be a very good Tuesday evening. On Wednesday is a very controversial event that some of you have heard about – in America we want to have everything that everyone else has. There is an American avatar, who calls himself Bubba Free John, and who is at the very least gifted in theater. He has been able to sustain a theater for years of spiritual teaching and he has hundreds of people around him, some of whom I know and respect. They are going to be coming to the city to show some films about Bubba and talk about his new book. They have invited me to come down and be a gadfly. I do not know if you know the word. Socrates called himself a gadfly who would sit and bite and ask difficult questions. So, they asked me to come along too and be critical and ask difficult questions and they are going to answer them. It is an interesting issue, an American spiritual master who proclaims himself to be a teacher of the level of Krishna or Buddha and who sustains a very intense level of theater about this. It is a very important cultural and spiritual issue. That is going to be Wednesday night at the East West Center for Holistic Health, which is at 141 5th Avenue at 21st Street, 8th Floor at 7:30pm. Some people may find it interesting on many levels. And finally, the last thing is that this Tuesday evening from 5-7:30, Paul Gorman and I are going to be together again talking about the station and maybe raising some funds. Those who have not listened, may be interested to know that a couple of times we came on the air and asked people for support and raised over $4,000 on just two programs of *In the Spirit*. There was a tremendous response from the audience. If you did not happen to be there or have a chance to pledge and would like to, it might be fun to listen to us this Tuesday night from 5 – 7:30pm. Paul Gorman and I will talk about the station and take some phone calls and talk in a kind of Sunday morning style during the week, which is something unheard of. They must be getting desperate. Okay, that is about all I have to say. I am going to play some music first and clear the atmosphere. Again, we have Maezumi Roshi from the LA Zen Center and we are going to spend a couple hours in a really deep inquiry. I urge you to call your friends who would be interested and do stay tuned. If you missed any of those announcements, the *In the Spirit* number is 966-0554. We will be back in a moment with the Roshi.

[music interval]

> "About my father, ever since I was very young he was almost constantly constructing, building portions of the temples, and in accord with these buildings he moved around trees, rocks, and for us it was almost unnecessary to move trees, rocks, and bushes, but he was constantly doing that. All the time, we asked him, "Why? Why do you do that?" And what he used to tell us is that trees and rocks like to be appreciated. Be kind to them. It was that kind of a teaching. Not only inanimate things like trees, but people too. We should be kind to people."

LEX: Maezumi Roshi, you have had three major teachers in Zen, you might say Dharma fathers. One of them is actually your father, your physical father. We were hoping you would say something about these three teachers to give us a sense of what a real process of transmission is. Maybe we could begin with your own father, Baian Hakujun Kuroda. How did he train you in Zen? What kind of things as a young boy did you feel you were getting from him?

ROSHI: First of all, I should like to express my thanks to you, Lex, your generosity, kindness, warm friendship. It is very much appreciated. Aaaah... I have been in this country for some time, over 20 years. Number of times (laughs) I was asked about my father. Each time I was very reluctant (more laughing) to talk about that. It is kind of strange Japanese custom. We do not talk much about our own side. Beside these three teachers, I studied under other teachers, such as the Chief of my Monastery, where I was 20 some years ago, whom I like very much and I admired. And there was another teacher who was at the time in charge of the downtown Los Angeles Temple as the Bishop. And I learned many things from many teachers. But somehow, I can say that I learned from my father the most perhaps; being together the longest is one reason. And also, what I have learned is one thing, and how he showed us to live life, that is another. To that extent, I learned a lot from my father.

LEX: Can you give us just a small incident?

ROSHI: For example, ever since I was very young he was almost constantly constructing, building portions of the temples, and in accord with these buildings he moved around trees, rocks, and for us it was almost unnecessary to move trees, rocks, and bushes, but he was constantly doing that. All the time, we asked him, "Why? Why do you do that?" And what he used to tell us is that trees and rocks like to be appreciated. Be kind to them. It was that kind of a teaching. Not only inanimate things like trees, but people too. We should be kind to people. And almost constantly we learned from him.

LEX: That kindness is reflected a little bit in your LA Zen Center. They have a whole block in LA. And they invite everyone into their community – old people, young people – and they have a clinic there and there is a lot of kindness expressed in that community. Maybe that is your father's transmission coming through. Can you remember him giving you direct teaching about Buddha dharma that was powerful?

ROSHI: Yes. Just before I came to this country – I was appointed at the end of 1955, then I came here in 1956 – prior to my coming to this country, I had dharma teaching from my father.

LEX: Is it possible to share anything of what he said to you, sending his son off to carry the Dharma to the West.

ROSHI: Hard to say...that is what I have done to Sensei here in this country.

LEX: So, he gave you his wholehearted permission to teach the dharma?

ROSHI: Yes.

LEX: Is he pleased with your work? Does he think you are being kind enough to things over here?

ROSHI: Now, that I do not know. (both laugh)

LEX: I was talking to the Roshi before the program and I wanted him to give us a few examples of transmission and the feeling of transmission, because Zen is not some sort of isolated insight; it is something that is very carefully prepared. Each generation prepares it carefully and hands it on to the next, as Roshi said. From maybe at least three, and more enlightened Zen teachers, he's received this transmission. Can you give us more stories, perhaps about Koryo Roshi?

ROSHI: I started to study with Koryo Roshi since I was 16, 17, I do not remember exactly, but the first session I had with him was about that age. At that time, he was very young, perhaps before 50, which are perhaps as a roshi the most vigorous kind of years. I have many memories being with him, but again his general way to treat the people is a very interesting one. It was a favorite of his to say "ahh, sooo," which literally means "is that so." At that time about 12 students were living in the dormitory where he resides and time to time, see, we are allowed to go and talk to him, and we thought in the way of being young and college students, we are proud of what we say (laughing) and we think we are very smart and he listens, see, to what we say, and he says, "ahh, sooo" It sounds like he really believes us, see? (laughing hard) Later on, thinking of these incidents, I felt almost like bashful. He seemed to understand our position, and he treated older people the same way. There, I saw another side of his wonderful attainment around the young and old being very equally treated.

LEX: You were 16 or 17 at that time, and you had become a monk earlier – when you were 12 or something like that? Were you very eager to attain enlightenment at 16 or 17? Were you extremely intense in your practice?

ROSHI: Up and down. (laughing a lot)

LEX: Sometimes, did you feel like an ordinary 16 year old boy, that you would like to just leave the temple and just have fun in the world?

> "In a way, our practice is an endless practice. It is simply because life itself is an endless, boundless thing and our practice is life, living itself. So, it is such a rich thing, almost indescribably rich here – we constantly learn, constantly create all kinds of things."

ROSHI: I was very much interested in literature, in poetry, and also criticism, and one time I intended to be like a critic; it did not last so long. (laughing).

LEX: Did the Roshi....was he very demanding in his training with you, or did he say, "Well, just take your time, you have plenty of time to be enlightened." What sort of attitude did the Koryo Roshi have about that?

ROSHI: He spoke as if enlightenment was not the major requirement.

LEX: Your father seemed like such a gentle, compassionate man, but the other roshi seemed a little more demanding somehow.

ROSHI: Yes, my study with Koryo tended to be more demanding, but certain aspects of Soto practice in a way are very demanding too. But as a teacher, when I compare these 3 teachers, I think Koryo Roshi was perhaps the most demanding (laughs).

LEX: Can you give an example of that? Of just one demand he put on you, just one concrete example?

ROSHI: For example, having *doksan*. Doksan means a sort of personal, private interview, and he is going to really urge you to bring up an answer. Sometimes it is extremely painful. Like during a *sesshin* (laughs), you are forced to give an answer.

LEX: Is it too private or can you tell us any of these conversations that you had with him?

ROSHI: For example, the famous *koan*, "Has a dog Buddha nature, or not?" This koan is very demanding.

LEX: If those of you who are listening could see this on television now, you could perhaps get a more direct idea of what we are talking about. Roshi is sitting here in the studio on a little folding chair, sitting cross-legged and he has a tremendous presence about him that has just been built up through all these transmissions through all these teachers. What would Koryo Roshi do or say if your answer was not adequate?

ROSHI: Does not say much, that is the problem. (both laugh heartily)

LEX: The problem with you also! (still laughing)

ROSHI: Yasutani Roshi has another kind of aspect. We have been talking about general characteristics. Maybe I can say something about Yasutani Roshi. I have known him in his later years. He died when he was 88. I think I have first known him when he was 76 years old, something like that, see? And mostly I was amazed from time to time because he was almost constantly writing. He published a number of books. The last minute, just before he died, he was also writing, got heart attack, and practically died having pen in his hand.

LEX: I know that some people who are listening may be familiar with Yasutani Roshi's writing, which is printed in *The Three Pillars of Zen*, I think a Beacon paperback. There are some introductory lectures on Zen that are very beautiful there, and for years I have been reading those and so I feel very personal, close to the Yasutani Roshi. I understand that when you came to him, you started your koan practice all over again and went through the entire training again with him. Did he ask you to do this, or did you feel that after all these teachers and transmissions you wanted to go through the whole thing again to make sure it was absolutely.....

ROSHI: (interrupting) Yes, I wanted to. Since I came to this country fairly young, I did not finish studying with Koryo Roshi either and about 10 years in between with Koryo Roshi so it was to me quite natural. I thought it was a good idea to study under Yasutani Roshi and I tried to make opportunity to study as much as possible.

LEX: It is so good for us to hear this, Roshi, because perhaps something in the American temperament feels that maybe you do not have to study at all but if you do study, it should be just a few years and that you should be finished. The fact that you, even in this advanced stage, having so many teachings and receiving so much, that you wanted to start your studies all over again with this great Yasutani Roshi, it is an example to all of us to continue studying. (laughs) You say that Koryo Roshi was very stern and demanding and your father....

ROSHI: Koryo Roshi was somewhat like a sharp dagger.

LEX: Like a pick-axe?

ROSHI: Yasutani Roshi was like a sword. And Koryo Roshi was like an axe.

LEX: It is a dangerous thing to study Zen (both laugh). I can somehow feel that Yasutani Roshi like a sword somehow just cuts through space. It doesn't even enter the earth. You don't dig with the sword, you don't cut trees down with a sword. With a sword you're just swinging through open space. Yasutani Roshi is that way. Tremendously pure, not contacting any dharmas anywhere type of thing.

ROSHI: That's very true. Even though his appearance is rather gentle. Perhaps many Americans know Yasutani Roshi because of his 10 years' visit to this country. But his appearance is very gentle but his writings, his wisdom is very, very sharp. That's the most I appreciate studying with him.

LEX: So, when you were involved in a personal interview with him he would be very, very sharp in his perception of your answers and your understanding. An ideal person to finish your training with it would seem to me.

ROSHI: Perhaps you're right. To that extent I was very lucky.

LEX: It was like his guidance brought you through these different teachers.

ROSHI: And a wonderful thing too about Yasutani Roshi, he also had two teachers he studied from. Of course, he had many teachers, but two major teachers. One was a Soto teacher and another was a Roshi. He also was a Soto Roshi but he studied with Rinzai Roshi, Duktan Roshi, so besides this very intensive practice he was wonderful scholar, too. He taught at Kyoto University. Yasutani Roshi also received and studied with a wonderful Roshi of the Soto school, and also Rinzai School.

[music interval]

LEX: It's an important thing for Americans to hear at this point that scholarship and deep understanding of a tradition goes along with Zen as well as flower-arranging, or archery, or anything. And in the LA Zen Center they're starting a small, I guess you should call it a University, because it's going to be universal in its teachings, but it's a small college which eventually people will be able to study various aspects of spiritual traditions and culture. I think Maezumi Roshi and the LA Zen Center represent a new phase in the development of American Zen. It's very auspicious that we should have Maezumi Roshi this morning. This is the first time he's given a public talk in the East Coast. And I'd like to remind you that you are listening to *In the Spirit* and we're talking with Maezumi Roshi, the founder of the LA Zen Center. He's going to be giving a talk tomorrow evening at the Japan House at 333 East 47th Street. And again, next Saturday, he'll be giving a talk at the Universalist Church at 8:pm. That's at 4 West 76th Street. I urge everyone who's listening to come and give a loving welcome to Maezumi Roshi and let him see that this New York City is a very friendly place where people are interested in the deepest kind of inquiry, most authentic kind of spiritual practice.

I think we've heard from discussing with the Roshi about his background and his extensive training that this is what we have to look for in a spiritual teacher. Just flashes of insight are not enough. I want to mention that the LA Center publishes a very fine group of books. They are called *On Zen Practice*, Volume 1," *On Zen Practice*, Volume Two, and are paperbacks. There's a small manual on Zen, *Forget the Self*, and then another book called *The Hazy Moon of Enlightenment*, including some of the dharma discussions between Bernie Glassman Sensei and some of the students of the LA Zen Center. Very revealing conversations between western students and a western teacher. And then finally, there is a book called *The Way of Everyday Life*, which Maezumi Roshi has just published. It is a very beautiful book. All come in paperback and are available in good spiritual bookstores in the City.

LEX: Roshi, I want to ask you about something that interests me very much. I think it interests everyone who hears it. The moment you hear this you cannot help but be interested, it is the very deep teaching of the Zen tradition that it shares with other traditions: that the highest goal of life or the highest truth, however one wants to put it, already exists, already is fully expressed by the way we are now. We don't have to wait until our civilization becomes more advanced – for a thousand years when there's no more war or anything like that. We don't have to go to another planet. We don't have to necessarily meet any tremendously powerful person who will bless us. But really right now everyone, so-called ordinary people, have this completeness of truth. Can you say something about that and some of the problems of understanding it correctly?

ROSHI: As you say, the most important issues or matters as being, as far as we understand, are always right here and right now in one's self, not somewhere else, sometime else, or by someone else.

LEX: But the thing is that not only is the concern or the problem here and now, but the solution is already here and now. Is this true, and in which case, why do we necessarily have to practice Zen?

ROSHI: If we suddenly realize what we are this very moment, at this very space being existing as I am, if everybody knew, then no practice would be necessary.

LEX: Is there any way not to know what it really is? Isn't our ordinary knowing already that?

ROSHI: Yes, in a way we are wonderfully complete absolute beings and yet because of the lack of the awareness or wisdom, somehow, we create all sorts of difficulties.

LEX: We all have to be honest, speaking for myself, that we all have problems and difficulties that we create, but if we think that somehow we have to get over these difficulties and create something which would be the solution, then it becomes like an endless problem. How can you ever get over all the difficulties? But if you know that in the long run even these difficulties are already a completeness here, then one could have a lot of courage to go on and practice.

ROSHI: In a way, our practice is an endless practice. It is simply because life itself is an endless, boundless thing and our practice is life, living itself. So, it is such a rich thing, almost indescribably rich here – we constantly learn, constantly create all kinds of things. And that is why we say in Buddhism there are three treasures. And I think these three treasures are the most important regardless whether it is Zen Buddhism or Mahayana. And what are these three treasures? One is a Buddha Treasure, the second one is Dharma Treasure, and the third one, Sangha Treasure. And we can say these three treasures – we can appreciate them as they relate to the individual's life and the life of the community, life of even the country or the life of everything else. Well, what is this Buddha treasure? Some people think Buddhism is idol worship. (laughs)

LEX: Or, idle, "i – d – l – e," sitting around, idle worship. (both laugh)

ROSHI: But it is not true, see. Buddha treasure is The Supreme Way, or The Supreme Wisdom, or Supreme Enlightenment. Wisdom itself is a Buddha treasure, or the way Enlightenment is itself a treasure.

LEX: So, could you say that a Catholic priest or a Jewish rabbi could have this Buddha treasure?

ROSHI: Why not?

LEX: So, it is not limited to one group of people?

ROSHI: I don't think so. Being Jewish or being Christian, it's got to be enlightenment. And dharma, the Dharma Treasure — everything is, in a way, the Dharma. Of course, in the narrow sense, the Buddha's teaching is the Dharma, but here, in this case, the dharma is everything else. Everything in life is dharma. Then actually, life is like Buddha Treasure itself and I see living more like Dharma. Then the life and living is a Sangha, the har-

ADVAITA-SATYA-AMRITAM 47

mony. Then we can extend this basic principle into the larger scale of life.

LEX: The question still remains though, if we have these treasures of life and harmony, then we have everything. What is the need to practice?

ROSHI: Same thing. Okay, you may have lots of jewels, like a wonderful diamond. If you put it somewhere else and don't use it, don't appreciate it, then it becomes useless.

LEX: But don't people use their life every day and don't they really appreciate it?

ROSHI: If a diamond is in a drawer, it's not going to be appreciated in a favorable, adequate way.

LEX: Last week, when I was talking to Bernie Glassman Sensei, who is a western successor of Maezumi Roshi, I asked him to explain what was the sense of keeping a kosher house, like I am asking you what is the sense of practice or doing certain formal things. And he answered, "appreciation." Just a deeper and deeper appreciation of the sources of life and the modes of life that we experience.

ROSHI: And also, the process of pushing up, too.

LEX: What was that?

ROSHI: For example, a diamond. First it is covered by something else so that the outside is supposed to be taken off. Even the inside would be cut right and polished right, otherwise it won't be appreciated. So, this is an analogy. Analogy doesn't cover everything.

LEX: I was about to object. (both laugh) But it seems to me that in the human being, the body, the mind, the awareness, everything is already on the surface. You don't need to clear anything off, you don't need to cut anything. It seems to me that human awareness is already complete and full and so is life itself, although I grant that we all have lots of problems.

ROSHI: We don't think in that way. For example, we have in our tradition what are called 3 poisons. There are 3 kinds of poisons which affect life unfavorably: greed, anger, and folly or ignorance.

LEX: But these 3 poisons are something coming from the outside. We don't have poison in our body. We have to be bitten by a snake in order to get poison in us. I mean the nature of consciousness itself doesn't have that poison in it, does it?

ROSHI: Since it is not used in the right way, it becomes poisonous.

LEX: Ahhh.

ROSHI: Like medicine.

LEX: I see.

ROSHI: Actually, it is not a poison, it is a very virtuous aspect of life, but because of misuse and abuse of it, the good thing affects the body and mind unfavorably.

LEX: So, we have this fullness of life but we misuse it. That makes more sense to me because it means you don't have to scrape anything off it or cut it in some way, but you should use it correctly instead of misusing it.

ROSHI: So why do we misuse it? Because we are ignorant. So, it is a kind of interesting word, ignorance. In Chinese we write it, "no light, dark, darkness," see? Of course, the opposite of ignorance is wisdom. So how do we acquire wisdom, or how can we use wisdom which is already innate in us?

LEX: I feel that innateness is important to stress because suppose you asked someone, "what's 2 plus 2?" They immediately say, "4." The answer springs to them with a lot of clarity and immediacy. You could say that is a simple thing but it is a rudimentary form of wisdom. If you ask someone about whether selfishness is a good thing, immediately, most people, unless they are very sick or distorted, would say "No, selfishness is not a good thing." It springs up immediately. They don't have to be some advanced people who are doing a lot of zazen or anything. It's there, right on the surface, but strangely enough somehow all these pure impulses and insights we misuse. I know myself, I could say, "Yes, selfishness is bad," and the next moment I find myself being selfish.

ROSHI: That's very true.

[music interval]

LEX: I'm pursuing just a little bit of this kind of conversation with Roshi because, first of all, he's a very generous man to allow me to talk freely with him in this way. Maybe a more traditional Zen Roshi would not allow this kind of freedom. Maybe I would be struck by the stick by this time. It's very kind of you to let me just engage you this way in conversation, and really pressing. It's interesting that American culture is this way. You must run across many students who press this way, whereas maybe in a traditional setting in Japan you don't – you're lucky if you even speak to the Roshi much less ask him questions like this and push your own point of view. Do you think there is any value in this kind of discussion?

ROSHI: (quickly) Definitely. (both laugh)

LEX: This kind of intimacy, we're so grateful for – Maezumi Roshi has really adopted our culture. He's been here for 20 years. His wife is an American. He really has accepted and blended into our culture while still carrying the rich transmission of everything he's learned and everything of the Japanese culture. It makes a new combination. I just don't think in the past of Zen that you could hear this kind of frank conversation between an advanced teacher and someone who is interested. It is a great freedom I think we have in our culture.

VEDANTA 101: Spiritual Discrimination

Just as one cannot be a Buddhist unless one accepts the truth of suffering, and one cannot formally and effectively enter the spiritual pathway until one finds a guru and receives initiation, so too, in Vedanta, one cannot make progress along the spiritual pathway until the principle of *viveka* — discrimination between the real and the unreal — is implemented into one's practice. Maya is too deceptive, and the human mind too given to complacency and prevarication, for it to be otherwise. What is more, this world, its people, its societies, and its conventions, all thrive upon relativity, and leave Reality out of the picture. To love God over Mammon, then, is a rarety here. Thus, this age will require the healthiest spiritual tool known to mankind over the ages: *viveka*.

"Ignorance persists in the absence of discriminative wisdom."
Sri Ramachandra

The essential mainstay of Vedanta is the practice of spiritual discrimination. This is the way to methodically counteract *Vivarta*, discussed in Nectar issue 32. One of the great scriptures of the Advaita Vedanta school is the *Vivekachudamani*, the Crest Jewel of Discrimination by Shankaracharya. Why is discrimination the crest jewel? Because there is no destruction of ignorance without it. In the first few verses of this work, Shankara forcefully states that it is not by mere recitation of scripture, nor by rituals, wealth, progeny, or work, that liberation can be realized, but only by knowledge – direct perception – of one's identity with the *Atman*, the true Self/Soul. Ignorance of our identity as Atman is based in substituting everything else in place of the Atman: body, gender, occupation, emotions, mental states, intellect, ego, etc. Within the *Vivekachudamani*, Shankara assembles a veritable Vedantic tool box of ways to practice discrimination between the Atman and everything else. As there are various ways to express these two, let us begin with listing some of these, with commentary.

The Eternal and the Noneternal

When we speak of discrimination as a spiritual practice it means to perceive the distinction between the Eternal and the non-Eternal. This expression is the actual translation of a quintessential Sanskrit phrase for this practice: *Nitya-anitya vastu viveka*. *Nitya* means eternal, *anitya* means noneternal, *vastu* means between the two, and *viveka* means discrimination. By Eternal, is meant That which transcends the three phases of time, past, present, and future. The noneternal, therefore, have beginnings, middles, and endings. God/Self is eternal, and everything else is noneternal.

The Real and the Unreal

Next, we must discern the difference between the Real and the unreal. Sri Krishna states in chapter two of the *Bhagavad Gita*, *"The unreal has no existence; the Real never ceases to be. The truth about both has been realized by the seers."* The Real is existence itself. The unreal, which comes in and out of existence, borrows the appearance of existence from the Real, just as a mirage borrows its existence from the hot ground.

Another famous verse comes from the *Upanisads*: "Lead us *from untruth to Truth, from darkness to Light, from the illusion of death to realization of Eternal life."* Frequently, this verse is also translated, *"Lead us from the unreal to the Real."* Interestingly, the Sanskrit words for existence (*bhava*) and truth (*sat*) are both often translated into English as "Real," and there is much significance to this. What is it that is always Existent and always True? There is a notion current today that everyone has their own truth and there is no such thing as an absolute truth. This would be the natural conclusion for those who have never transcended matter, let alone concepts. But the seers of India and the exceptional saints and sages of other traditions have all realized an ultimate Existence, an ultimate Truth that is never nonexistent and never untrue. When all else passes out of time, or has its validity altered by location, time, and circumstance, That which is left is the True and the Real.

The Unchanging and the Changing

Further, there is perceiving the distinction between the Unchanging and the changing. This discrimination is based on the fact that movement can only be recognized by something that is moving slower, and the logical necessity that there is something that is unmoving. We have to think more deeply than the observation that we are changing all the time and witnessing other changes. What is it within us that knows the changes of body, mind, intellect, and ego? An astronomer friend once described his "ah ha!" moment when he understood this Vedantic discrimination. He was at a planetarium in Los Angeles watching the big pendulum clock made from a multistorey cable with a heavy weight at the end knock down the pins set around in a circle. Nothing but the motion of the earth was moving the cable and weight. As this man watched, he contemplated the issue of the earth seeming to be stationary even though it rotates and moves around the sun. So the really stationary phenomena would be the universe, but scientists know the universe is also moving. What is still enough to detect that? His reasoning went outward as far as he could go until a transcendent unchanging Reality was revealed – one that transcended the duality of outward and inward, what to speak of changing and Unchanging.

The Seer and the Seen

Next there is the difference between the Seer and the seen. This discrimination is based on the fact that the seer cannot be the seen; the one who sees an object is not that object. That we mix these two up constantly was observed by the ancient Seers/Rishis. We do this every time we say or think, "I am hungry, happy; I'm a female or male, a mother or father; I am rich or poor," etc. If I see my hunger, then I must be something different from that. If I see my gender, I must be something other than that, and so forth. Each of us has been seeing everything inside and outside "us," including when we are awake and when we are asleep. Further, that seer within us has always been the same, despite seeing changes of infancy to old age, changes of mood, intelligence, health, etc. For that Seer, all things inside and outside are the seen.

Consciousness and Matter

Next, there is the difference between Consciousness and matter. This discrimination focuses on facing up to the fact that Consciousness, a.k.a. Spirit, Soul, or Atman, is not matter and shares none of the properties of matter, such as manifestation and non-manifestation, mass and weight, dimensions, changes in time and location. Further, matter is always a compound, whether of atomic/gross/physical elements, or their subtle counterparts in the realm of thought. In contrast, Consciousness (Awareness, not thinking consciousness as in the activities of the mind and brain), is not a compound. It is the indivisible, self-effulgent Awareness that precedes all cognition.

The Sentient and the Insentient

Then, there is the difference between the Sentient and the insentient. This discrimination is similar to the one above, but with the emphasis on the fact that matter is not sentient, is not self-aware, and that the ultimate Seer is the sole Sentient Principle illumining everything else — including the mind and intellect. It is self-effulgent, needing no other light to reveal It. Instead, It is *"That one Light shining by which all else shines,"* as the *Upanisad* states. All vehicles of Intelligence, such as senses, mind, intellect, and ego, only borrow their intelligence from the Sentient Seer, just like the moon shines by the light of the sun. The insentient includes matter, energy, and thought.

The Self and the Nonself

Then comes the distinction between Self and the non-Self. This discrimination naturally calls forth all the Vedantic teachings concerning the various coverings over the Atman, the true Self. In the *Vivekachudamani*, Shankara goes through the gross, subtle, and causal bodies and their association with the states of waking, dreaming, and dreamless sleep. He also takes us through the five *koshas** or sheaths apparently covering the Atman and obscuring Its oneness with Brahman. All these bodies, states, and sheaths, which consist of elements, senses, subtle elements, mind, ego, intellect, cosmic mind, and unmanifested Nature (matter, Prakriti), are the nonself. The true Self, which is the Unchanging, Eternal, Sentient Seer that is pure Consciousness, is the substratum upon which all these appear. And falsely identifying with them is the cause of bondage and suffering. *[See "Adhara, the System of the Five Koshas," *Nectar*, issue 1]

The Eternal Subject and the Object

Next is the difference between the Eternal Subject and the object. This discrimination follows on the heels of the last, for it emphasizes the need to cease false identification of the Subject (the Seer, the Self) with the object. *"Knowing oneself to be the Subject, the witness of the intellect and its operations, reject the idea that the Self is other than the Subject by identifying the 'I' with That (the witness/subject)."* (Adhyatma Upanisad)

The Soul and Nature

Finally comes the distinction between the Soul and nature. This discrimination is really the same as between the Self and the non-Self, for the non-Self is, precisely, Nature. We must understand that in Indian philosophy and cosmology, nature includes not just what our external senses perceive but everything the mind can perceive or conjure up at individual, collective, and cosmic levels, on up to the Cosmic Mind and the unmanifested Nature (*Prakriti*) from which it all comes spilling forth. Nature/Prakriti includes the physical, mental, and causal states – all the realms of cause and effect. The Soul is simply other than all this, and when this is realized as a direct experience, not simply an intellectual glimpse, all ignorance and suffering come to an end. Akin to waking up from a dream, this is the ultimate waking — waking up from the waking state!

Devotion to Discrimination

Devotion to discrimination, then, means constantly applying any one of these discriminations. This must be done during formal sitting practice, where time is allotted to contemplating these distinctions and feeling the presence of the unchanging Seer/Self/Soul, etc., while examining the limitations and insentiency of the seen/objects/non-Self, nature etc. This practice, over time, leads to mental balance, and increases one's ability to employ this discrimination in daily activities and situations.

One might ask, how can we live this way without appearing aloof, distant, and uncaring of others? On the contrary, discrimination leads to calm detachment, through which we are able to offer selfless service and love. Our patience and forbearance is strengthened via discrimination, and our capacity to serve the true Self in others gains momentum. Further, we need not cater to those who thrive on drama and want us to emote with them. This is not spiritually healthy for them or for any true practitioner. As Swami Ashokananda once expressed in a lecture: upon entering seriously into spiritual life, one ceases to be the life of the party. So be it!

Discriminating Youth

In the case of our children, we show our love and concern best by teaching them to discriminate. In simple ways suitable to their understanding, we must do this to save them the suffering that comes with lack of self-control, emotionalism, and fear. Loss of fear is one of the tremendous results of this practice that makes the distinction between the eternal Self and the body-mind complex. Further, teaching our children discrimination leads to spiritual freedom, which is the greatest gift we can offer them. And one of the concomitants of doing this is that we ourselves must set the example! Our own discrimination strengthens in the process.

MEDITATION

May we always and ever meditate upon the radiant effulgence of the Supreme Being, abiding in our hearts and minds eternally

May that one, blessed Presence guide and protect us, and protect the Three Worlds

Om Peace, Peace, Peace
May Peace be unto us
may Peace be unto all

"I have met with great sages indeed! It is all very wonderful, and in this atheistic age, they are a towering representation of marvelous power born of bhakti and yoga. Unless one is face to face with the life of such men, faith in the scriptures does not grow in all its real integrity. They remain immersed in meditation and samadhi but talk to others when they come out. Such sweetness of speech one seldom comes across. They will receive you most warmly. And even if one can't have their company, no trouble taken for the sake of such great souls ever goes unrewarded."

ADVAITA-SATYA-AMRITAM

SRV Associations — Babaji's Teaching Schedule, 2018

SRV Hawai'i Administrative Office PO Box 1364 Honoka'a, HI 96727	SRV Associations' website: www.srv.org email: srvinfo@srv.org Phone: 808-990-3354	SRV Oregon 1922 SE 42nd Ave., Portland, OR 97215 Ph: 503-774-2410	SRV San Francisco 465 Brussels Street San Francisco, CA 94134 Ph: 415-468-4680

February, 2018

SRV San Francisco (Meditation, 6 to 7 am)
2/9   Fri   7:00pm   Arati/Satsang with Babaji
2/10 Sat   9:30am   Class: Amrita Bindu Upanisad
             7:00pm   **Sri Ramakrishna Birth Puja/Sivaratri**
2/11 Sun   9:30am   Class: Amrita Bindu Upanisad

SRV Oregon (Call for meditation times)
2/15 - 2/19   SRV Winter Retreat, Seattle, WA
2/21 Wed 7:00pm   Vedanta 101, with Annapurna Sarada
2/23 Fri   7:00pm   Satsang with Babaji
2/24 Sat   9:30am   Class: Adhyatma Upanisad
             6:00pm   **Sri Ramakrishna Birth Puja**
2/25 Sun   9:30am   Class: Adhyatma Upanisad

SRV Seattle Retreat, 2/15 - 2/19, Seattle, WA
Subject: Sri Ramakrishna & Universality
(arrive Thursday night 15th, depart Monday 19th at noon)
For details, see Retreat Pages

May, 2018

SRV San Francisco (Meditation, 6 to 7 am)
5/11 Fri   7:00pm   Arati/Satsang
5/12 Sat   9:30am   Class: Amrita Bindu Upanisad
             7:00pm   SRV Puja
5/13 Sun   9:30am   Class: Amrita Bindu Upanisad

SRV Oregon (Call for meditation times)
5/16 Wed 7:00pm   Principles of the Upanisads, with Anurag
5/18 Fri   7:00pm   Satsang with Babaji
5/19 Sat   9:30am   Class: Akshi Upanisad
             6:00pm   SRV Puja, Siva Puja
5/20 Sun   9:30am   Class: Akshi Upanisad
5/23 Wed 7:00pm   Principles of the Upanisads, with Anurag
5/24 - 5/28   Memorial Day Weekend Retreat

Memorial Day Weekend Retreat — 5/24 - 28
Subject: Vedanta & Buddhism:
Teachings of Vedavyasa, Buddha, Shankara, & Nagarjuna
Location: Windwood Waters (Wind River Region)
(arrive Thursday evening 24th, depart Monday 28th at noon)
For details, see Retreat Pages

Visit srv.org for all retreat details
Weekend Classes webcasted, 9:30 am to 12:30 pm, Pacific Time

SRV Hawaii Swamiji Guru Purnima Retreat
Big Island, Summer, 7/27 - 7/31
Subject: The Three Pillars: Sankhya, Yoga, & Vedanta

August/September, 2018

SRV San Francisco (Meditation, 6 to 7 am)
8/30 Fri   SRV SF Summer Retreat Begins at Foresthill, CA

SRV American River Retreat over Janmashtami
August. 30th, eve - Sept 3rd, noon – Foresthill, CA
Subject: The Two Divine Songs (Gitas) of Sri Krishna
Plus: Chanting, Memorization, & Discourse on select Stotrams
(arrive Thursday night 30th, depart Monday noon 9/3)
For details, see Retreat Pages

SRV Oregon (Call for meditation times)
9/8   Sat   9:30am   Class: Akshi Upanisad
             6:00pm   SRV Puja, Siva Puja
9/9   Sun   9:30am   Class: Akshi Upanisad
9/12 Wed 7:00pm   Vedanta 101, with Anapurna Sarada
9/14 Fri   6:00pm   Open Seminar Satsang with Babaji
9/14 -16   Weekend Seminar

SRV Weekend Seminar with Satsang, 9/14 - 16
Subject: Jnanamritam Chalisa – "Like The Sky" Stotram
Friday Satsang at 6 pm, & 2 classes Sat., 2 classes Sun.
Singing, Discourse, Commentary, & Contemplation
on these 40 verses from the Avadhuta Gita

November/December, 2018

SRV San Francisco (Meditation, 6 to 7 am)
11/30 Fri 7:00pm   Arati/Satsang
12/1   Sat   9:30am   Class: Upanisad TBA
             7:00pm   **Sri Sarada Devi Puja**
12/2   Sun 9:30am   Class: Upanisad TBA

SRV Oregon (Call for meditation times)
12/7 Fri   7:00pm   Satsang with Babaji
12/8 Sat   9:30am   Class: Akshi Upanisad
             6:00pm   **Sri Sarada Devi Puja**
12/9 Sun   9:30am   Class: Akshi Upanisad
12/12 Wed 7:00pm   Vedanta 101, with Anapurna Sarada
12/13-12/17   Seattle Winter Retreat

SRV Winter Retreat — 12/13 - 12/17, Seattle, WA
Subject: The Seven Goddess Upanisads
Savitri Upanisad, with Yoga Kundalini Upanisad
(arrive Thursday evening 13th, depart Monday 17th at noon)
For details, see Retreat Pages

---

* **Vedanta for Teens & Children**
at SRV Oregon and SRV San Francisco
Contact Annapurna Sarada — Ph: 808-990-3354

SRV Associations — Babaji's Teaching Schedule, 2018
SRV Hawai'i Retreat Center & Ashram

Hawaii Winter Retreat
Title: Precipitous Ascent into Higher Awareness II
Location: Paauilo, Big Island of Hawaii
January 12th - 16th, 2018

Sunday Live Streaming Classes, 2:30 - 5:30pm
Hawai'i SRV Ashram   Directions: Call: 808-990-3354

- **With Form & Without Form**
  December 10, 17, 24, & 31st, 2017
- **Worship & Study of Siva & Shakti**
  January 14, 21, & 28th, 2018
- **The Secret of Spiritual Self-Storage**
  March 11, 18, & 25th
- **Transgression, Transmigration, Transformation, Transcendence, & Transparency**
  April 8, 15, 22, & 29th
- **Vedanta & Tibetan Buddhism**
  June 10, 17, & 24th
- **Suffering, Striving, & Samadhi**
  July 8, 15, & 22nd

Hawaii Summer Gurupurnima Retreat
Title: The Three Pillars — Sankhya, Yoga, & Vedanta
Location: Paauilo, Big Island of Hawaii
July 27th - 31st, 2018

- **Mantra, Karma, & Purification**
  August 5, 12, & 19th
- **Mahamaya & Maya: Intelligence vs. Matter**
  September 30 & October 7, 14th
- **Stages, Phases, Levels, & Connections**
  October 28, & November 4, 11, & 18th

Also, check www.srv.org for Hawaii retreats or see our Retreats Pages in the back of this issue
Sign up for:
- SRV Magazine: Nectar of Non-Dual Truth
- Raja Yoga email study with Babaji
- SRV's Facebook page
- SRV's YouTube channel: Teaching videos

SRV Hawai'i Administrative Office:
PO Box 1364
Honoka'a, HI 96727
Ph: 808-990-3354

SRV Associations' website:
www.srv.org
email:
srvinfo@srv.org

See our SRV Facebook Page facebook.com/srv.vedanta

SRV Associations Website
www.srv.org
srvinfo@srv.org

SRV On The Web
Visit www.srv.org to find:
SRV's Livestream Channel
Webcast Time Zone Schedule
SRV's YouTube Channel Class Series
- Advaita of the Avatars
- Devotion of Nonseparation
- The Wisdom Particle
- Non-Touch Yoga
- Shakta-Advaita-vada
- Food, Prana, & Sadhana
- Satsangs with Babaji

Explore our Website links to find:
- Sanskrit Chants to learn/practice
- Devotional Songs
- Audio Discourses

Teachings:
- Articles
- Raja Yoga Sutras Study
- SRV's Teachings for Youth/Children
- Podcasts

Magazine:
- Order back issues of Nectar
- View our online archive of Nectar
- Order back issues of Nectar

News & Events
- Mundamala – SRV's e-newsletter
  Full of teachings & current events

SRV Associations — Retreats for 2018

SRV Seattle Retreat
February 15th - 19th, 2018, Seattle, Washington
Retreat Topic: Sri Ramakrishna & Universality

The advent of Sri Ramakrishna in 1836 in India has ushered in an age that some have called "....the return of the *Satya Yuga*," or Age of Truth. Whatever the case historically or cosmically, what is certain is that an age where that long-awaited principle of Universality has made its auspicious appearance. More than just the insight that the different religious traditions of the world need to find peace and harmony with one another, the Great Master — who practiced so many of them Himself to reveal the open way to Truth — brought to light the fact that all religions, if sincerely practiced, lead to the same Goal of God-realization. How He accomplished this greatest of all miracles is a wonder.

SRV's late winter retreat in Seattle will concentrate on both the Great Master's method of revealing the Unity of all religious traditions, as well as teachings showing the many similarities between the world's religions — all based in Mother India's ancient and timeless scriptural proclamation from the Rig Veda, *"Ekam sat vipra bahudha vedanti, Truth is One, paths are many."*

"My mind is still floating in the luminous atmosphere which that wonderful man diffuses around him whenever and wherever he goes. And what is his religion? Ramakrishna Paramahamsa accepts all the doctrines, all the embodiments, usages, and devotional practices of every religious cult. Each in turn is infallible to him. He is an idolater, yet is a faithful and most devoted meditator on the perfections of the one formless, Infinite Deity, whom he terms Akhanda Satchidananda. His religion is not like the religion of ordinary Hindu monks. His religion means ecstasy; his worship means transcendental insight. But how is it possible that he has such a fervent regard for all? What is the secret of his singular eclecticism? To him each of these deities is a force, an incarnate principle, tending to reveal the supreme relation of the soul to that eternal and formless Being, who is Unchangeable." Pratap Chandra Majumdar

Location: Seattle, Washington **Arrival:** Thursday, February 15th, after dinner, by 9:00pm
Departure: Monday, February 19th, at 12:00 noon
Tuition (all inclusive): $450; students $200 **Registration:** Starts now. Tuition is due by February 1st
Financial hardship? Call 808-990-3354 **Register by email:** srvinfo@srv.org or by phone 808-990-3354

SRV Spring Retreat Over Memorial Day Weekend
May 24th – 28th, 2018, Wind River region, Stevenson, Washington
Subject: Vedanta & Buddhism (Teachings of Buddha, Gaudapada, Shankara, & Nagarjuna)

Out of Mother India has emanated a host of real religions and powerful philosophies, all bearing the distinctive markings of compassionate devotion and underlying nonduality. Two of these, most remarkable, are the ancient Vedanta and more recent Buddhism. Despite their orthodox and unorthodox headings they mirror each other, while simultaneously complementing one another as well.

In SRV's Spring retreat at Windwood Waters within view of the Columbia River Gorge in Washington state, dharma teachings from both religions/philosophies will reach the ears and enter the hearts of all who are in attendance.

Location: Windwood Waters retreat site near Stevenson, WA
Arrival: Thursday, May 24th, by 9:00 pm **Departure:** Monday, May 28th, 12:00 noon
Registration: Starts now. Tuition and lodging fees are due by May 7th
Register by email: srvinfo@srv.org or by phone 808-990-3354
Costs: Tuition and meals: $490; Students:: $275 (lodging additional) **Lodging:** private room single, $240; private room shared with 1 - 2 others, $160/person; Semi-private lodge sleeping, $120*; Tenting, $80* *bring bedding & towels

SRV American River Sri Krishna Janmashtami Retreat, 2018
August 30th – September 3rd, 2018, Foresthill, CA
• The Two Divine Songs (Gitas) of Sri Krishna
Plus: Chanting and Study of Select Stotrams

- Live in holy company for a few sacred days – meditating, studying, serving, and growing together.
- Each morning begins with chanting from the Bhagavad Gita prior to meditation.
- Daily classes include essential teachings of Yoga, Vedanta, Tantra, Buddhism, and Sankhya.
- Afternoons include explorations and swimming/sunning along the American River.
- Afternoon Chela Dharma class for teens and young adults.
- Evening devotions at the altar, chanting, meditation, and satsang.
- Spiritual Music Features

Location: Private land in Foresthill, California near the American River
Arrival: Arrive by 6pm, Thursday evening, August 30th
Last day of retreat: Monday, Sept 3rd (approximately noon, clean up follows)
Tuition: all inclusive Adults: $490, students: $225   Daily rate, $165/$130
Registration: starts now and tuition is due by August 15th
Register by email: srvinfo@srv.org or by phone 808-990-3354
Financial hardship? Call 808-990-3354 to discuss options

SRV Early Winter Retreat, 2018
December 13th – 17th, 2018, Location: Seattle, Washington
Subject: The Seven Goddess Upanisads: Part 4 — Savitri & Yoga Kundalini Upanisads

Divine Mother Upanisads remain overlooked and unnoticed among seekers of Truth. Two important scriptures will come to light on this retreat, revealing the Mother of the Universe as the infinite fount of all Wisdom.

Location: Seattle, Washington
Arrival: Thursday, December 13th after dinner, by 9:00pm
Departure: Monday, December 17th, 12:00 noon
Tuition (all-inclusive): Adults: $450: Students: $200
Registration: Tuition is due by December 1st
Financial hardship? Call 808-990-3354 to discuss options
Register by email: srvinfo@srv.org or by phone 808-990-3354

SRV Summer Seminar in 2018, Sept. 14 -16th, Portland, Oregon Ashram
Subject: Jnanamritam Chalisa — "Like The Sky" Stotram
Chanting, Discourse, Commentary, and Contemplation of these Forty Verses from the Avadhuta Gita

"I am the fire of nondual Wisdom that consumes the activities of the actionless Atman; I am the fire of nondual Wisdom that removes the sorrows of the sorrowless Atman; I am the nondual Wisdom that dissolves all the bodies of the bodiless Atman. I am Pure Existence, Wisdom, and Bliss, as boundless as the sky, infinite like space. I am the fire of nondual Wisdom that eradicates the sins of the sinless Atman; I am the fire of nondual Wisdom that renders extinct the attributes of the attributeless Atman; I am the fire of nondual Wisdom that strikes off the bonds of the unbound Atman. I am Pure Existence, Wisdom, and Bliss, as boundless as the sky, infinite like space."

Schedule: Friday, September 14th: 6:00 PM – Satsang
Saturday, Sept 15th: 6:00am – 5:00pm (meditation, breakfast, morning and afternoon classes, dinner)
Sunday, Sept 16th: 6:00am – 5:00pm (meditation, breakfast and morning class)
Accommodations: This is a non-residential seminar
Tuition: $260; student, $130
Register by email: srvinfo@srv.org or by phone 808-990-3354
Registration: Tuition due by Saturday, September 1st
Financial hardship? Call 808-990-3354 to discuss options
Contact us if you would like assistance with lodging. 808-990-3354 // srvinfo@srv.org

The "In The Spirit" Interviews of Lex Hixon

Lex Hixon

From the early 1970's on through the late 1980's, Lex Hixon hosted a radio program in New York City that was unprecedented in its depth, scope, insight and unique creativity. First entitled "In The Spirit," it also later appeared under the titles of "Body/Mind/Spirit," and "Spirit/Mind/Body."

On this long running inspirational program that spanned over two decades and which was duly sponsored in listener-supported fashion on WBAI Radio, Lex interviewed educators, healers, clergy, authors, artists, psychics, spiritual leaders and others.

As a list, the fruit of this selfless work reads like a comprehensive Who's Who of the spiritual, artistic and intellectual heart and mind of both Eastern and Western cultures. With subtle tenderness and insight, though never lacking the penetrating edge which makes for excellent broadcasting, Lex welcomed the orthodox and the unorthodox, the conservative and the radical, the famous and the obscure, the popular and the controversial, the powerful and the humble, the aggressive and the retiring.

Included in this copious series are interviews with gurus, yogis, swamis, priests, roshis, rabbis/rebbes, sheikhs, lamas, rinpoches, poets, musicians, psychics, occultists, authors, writers, teachers, politicians, businessmen and more.

- Over 325 Titles to choose from
- Individual CD's are available
- Trio sets
- Full set prices
- List of all titles available upon request
- Highest quality materials used

"IN THE SPIRIT" CD Trio Sets
Choice selections from the cassette series on CD

Buddhist
B1 - Tibetan
Dalai Lama
Kalu Rinpoche
Trungpa Rinpoche

B2 - Zen
Eido Roshi
Soen Roshi
Maesumi Roshi

B3 - American
Phillip Kapleau
Bernie Glassman
Robert Thurman

Christianity
C1 - Mother Teresa
Padre Pio
Meister Ekhart

Islam/Sufism
IS1 - Sheikh Muzaffer
Guru Bawa
Sheikh Nur Al Jerrahi

Judaism
J1 - Rabbi Shlomo Carlebach
Rebbe Gedalia
Rabbi Zalman Schachter

J2 - Rebbi Meyer Fund
Rabbi Dovid Din
Rabbi Lynn Gotleib

Lex Hixon
H1 - On the Haj
On the Karmapa
On Himself

Professors & Authors
PA1 - Huston Smith
Christopher Isherwood
Jack Cornfield

PA2 - David Spangler
Alan Watts
Alan Ginsberg

Shamanism/Amer. Indian
SI1 - Oh Shinnah
Dhani Thorna
Don Juan

Vedic
V1 - Sri Ramakrishna

V2 - Ramakrishna Order Swamis
Vivekananda
Nikhilananda
Prabhavananda

V3 - Swamis
Dayananda
Muktananda
Satchitananda

V4 - Special Luminaries
Ramana Maharshi
Sri Aurobindo
Krishnamurti

V5 - Spiritual Teachers
Meher Baba
Sri Chinmoy
Ram Das

V6 - Divine Mother of the Universe

Postal Orders: Jai Ma Music, PO Box 380, Paauilo, HI 96776
Email Orders: srvinfo@srv.org
Phone Orders: 808-990-3354
Website: www.srv.org

Advaita-satya-amritam

NECTAR
Of Non-Dual Truth

Donation/Order Form
Suggested donation $15 per issue

Nectar #33 is available for free if you write, email, or call for a copy by January 15, 2018.
Your generous donations make Nectar available to others.
Those who donate $15 or more for the next issue will be added our subscribers list.

- ☐ Please send me/my friend a free copy of the next issue of Nectar.
- ☐ Send me ____ copies to give to friends, Spiritual Centers, or a business of my choice. (fill out back of form)
- ☐ I want to make sure there are future issues of Nectar ($200 and up)

Nectar needs sustaining donors! ($500 and up) Your gift is tax-deductible.

Please fill out the back side of this form and mail it with your check to:
SRV Associations, PO Box 1364, Honokaa, HI 96727
MasterCard or Visa accepted • Make checks payable to: SRV Associations
808-990-3354 • srvinfo@srv.org • www.srv.org

#33

Advaita-satya-amritam

NECTAR
Of Non-Dual Truth

Donation/Order Form
Suggested donation $15 per issue

Nectar #33 is available for free if you write, email, or call for a copy by January 15, 2018.
Your generous donations make Nectar available to others.
Those who donate $15 or more for the next issue will be added our subscribers list.

- ☐ Please send me/my friend a free copy of the next issue of Nectar.
- ☐ Send me ____ copies to give to friends, Spiritual Centers, or a business of my choice. (fill out back of form)
- ☐ I want to make sure there are future issues of Nectar ($200 and up)

Nectar needs sustaining donors! ($500 and up) Your gift is tax-deductible.

Please fill out the back side of this form and mail it with your check to:
SRV Associations, PO Box 1364, Honokaa, HI 96727
MasterCard or Visa accepted • Make checks payable to: SRV Associations
808-990-3354 • srvinfo@srv.org • www.srv.org

#33

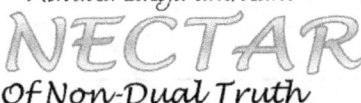

Advaita-satya-amritam

NECTAR
Of Non-Dual Truth

Donation/Order Form
Suggested donation $15 per issue

Nectar #33 is available for free if you write, email, or call for a copy by January 15, 2018.
Your generous donations make Nectar available to others.
Those who donate $15 or more for the next issue will be added our subscribers list.

- ☐ Please send me/my friend a free copy of the next issue of Nectar.
- ☐ Send me ____ copies to give to friends, Spiritual Centers, or a business of my choice. (fill out back of form)
- ☐ I want to make sure there are future issues of Nectar ($200 and up)

Nectar needs sustaining donors! ($500 and up) Your gift is tax-deductible.

Please fill out the back side of this form and mail it with your check to:
SRV Associations, PO Box 1364, Honokaa, HI 96727
MasterCard or Visa accepted • Make checks payable to: SRV Associations
808-990-3354 • srvinfo@srv.org • www.srv.org

#33

Your Information:
Name: _____
Address: _____
City, State, Zip: _____
Email: _____

Additional Address: (please use a sheet of paper for more addresses)
Name: _____
Address: _____
City, State, Zip: _____
Email: _____

Do you wish to pay by Mastercard or Visa?
Card No.: _____ Amount: _____
Exp. date: _____ Phone no.: _____
Signature: _____

Questions? call SRV Associations: 808-990-3354

Your Information:
Name: _____
Address: _____
City, State, Zip: _____
Email: _____

Additional Address: (please use a sheet of paper for more addresses)
Name: _____
Address: _____
City, State, Zip: _____
Email: _____

Do you wish to pay by Mastercard or Visa?
Card No.: _____ Amount: _____
Exp. date: _____ Phone no.: _____
Signature: _____

Questions? call SRV Associations: 808-990-3354

Your Information:
Name: _____
Address: _____
City, State, Zip: _____
Email: _____

Additional Address: (please use a sheet of paper for more addresses)
Name: _____
Address: _____
City, State, Zip: _____
Email: _____

Do you wish to pay by Mastercard or Visa?
Card No.: _____ Amount: _____
Exp. date: _____ Phone no.: _____
Signature: _____

Questions? call SRV Associations: 808-990-3354